for Melinda

Jason Sherman won the 1995 Governor-General's Literary Award for Drama for *Three in the Back, Two in the Head* (Playwrights Canada Press), which had its premiere at Tarragon Theatre in Toronto, in January, 1994, in a co-production with Necessary Angel Theatre in Toronto, and the National Arts Centre in Ottawa. It was produced by MCC Theatre, Off-Broadway in New York in May, 1996, and is scheduled for production in French, in Montreal, by Théâtre de la Manufacture in April, 1997.

The playwright's other works include the Chalmers Award-winning *The League of Nathans*, produced by Orange Dog Theatre in association with Theatre Passe Muraille, Toronto, 1991, and published by Scirocco Drama; and two plays for CBC Radio: "PMO" and "Patience". "Reading Hebron" will be produced at Factory Theatre in November, 1996.

He is also a critic, journalist and editor (two anthologies for Coach House Press: *Canadian Brash* and *Solo*). Jason Sherman has been playwright-in-residence at Tarragon Theatre since 1992.

"The Retreat" was developed through a playwright residency with Necessary Angel Theatre; the Tarragon Theatre Playwrights Unit, and the 1995 Alberta Theatre Projects *play*Rites festival. I am grateful to Richard Rose, Brian Quirt, Bob White, Don Kugler, Urjo Kareda, Andy McKim, Ian Prinsloo and, especially, Melinda Little, for their advice, generosity and patience.

— *Jason Sherr*

"The Retreat" was first produced by Tarragon Theatre, February 14 to March 17, 1996, Toronto with the following cast:

RACHEL BENJAMIN	*Sarah Oren*
DAVID FINE	*Joseph Zi*
JEFF BLOOM	*Pete* *t*
WOLF BENJAMIN	*Aron* *er*

Directed by Ian Prinsloo.
Set and costume design by Charlotte Dean.
Lighting by Andrea Lundy.
Stage manager - Fiona Jones.

The play is set in Toronto, and at an artists' retreat in the Can Rockies, in the autumn of 1993.

Running time - 2 hours, 15 minutes.

The spelling and punctuation in this play strictly adhere to   thor's instructions.

ACT ONE

1. RACHEL BENJAMIN's apartment, Toronto.

RACHEL   *(on the phone)* Don't tell me...don't tell me what I can't...I am their teacher. I am teaching them...no, not what to think, how to think...the diff...the difference...I don't care what the Parents Committee said, the Parents Comm...let me tell you about the Parents' Committee, Bernie: they're a bunch of spoon-fed, upper-middle-class Forest Hill Jews who pay lip service to every illegal, immoral act of the Israeli government, who...what? oh, that's...that's anti-Semitic...how?...how is that anti-Se...you see? Da, Dare to open your mouth, criticise and...Look. The class is called Israel Today, and what I said, what I said was: if these men, these Palestinian men, are terrorists, then why don't we call the Jewish settlers on the West Bank terrorists too?...well, I'm sorry the Lifkin boy went home in tears...if I knew he had a brother who lived on the West Bank, I...look, the only way we're gonna have peace is if...my God, I am sick to death of people blindly following this leader and that leader and the empty promises of a better life when the end result always and forever has been and will be deception, betrayal and misery...and *that* is why it's important for me to, yes, challenge these kids to think critically...I know they're thirteen years old, Bernie...well tha...that's why it's important for me, for us, to tell them, now...what did you say?...what did you say to me?...I know exactly what you *meant...I* don't have children, *that's* what you...look, we're going nowhere...we're...we're going in circles here, Bernie...you called me...do you have something to offer me?...Apologise or quit? That's my option? ...that is...that is...Stalin would have been proud of you, you and that *Parents'* Commitee...Bernie I, I have to go. I have to catch my flight...the retreat, the writer's retreat...look, give me the week...I'll call you when I get back...yeah...Shana Tova.

She hangs up.

2. Office of DAVID FINE, a film producer. Enter JEFF BLOOM.

JEFF	Fuck you doin?
DAVID	What's it look like? I'm packing.
JEFF	I can see that, where you going?
DAVID	The Retreat.
JEFF	The Re—No, no…you're not going…
DAVID	I'm gettin outta here.
JEFF	We've got to deal with Earl.
DAVID	Don't mention that name to me, okay? I am getting out of this miserable grey city, I'm gonna go climb a mountain, breathe fresh air, swim in water you can't develop photographs in. I am going to see if I can find a reason not to quit this piece of shit business, to be with people, young people, *real* people, actual human *beings,* who still have souls, who want to make movies, who want what I used to want.
JEFF	You're not going anywhere.
DAVID	I told you about this two months ago.
JEFF	Two months ago I didn't have Earl's agent on line three wanting to know if we're gonna commit.
DAVID	Fuck Earl.
JEFF	"Fuck Earl"?
DAVID	Did you read the script I left on your desk?
JEFF	Did I…What?

DAVID   I left a script on your desk. *""Zevi"*. One of the students wrote it: did you read it?

JEFF   Did I read it? Did I read a student script when we're about to lose—

DAVID   You didn't, did you? You don't care. You're not interested. See ya.

JEFF   David, don't...

DAVID   I'm not *inte*rested.

JEFF   For *fuck's* sake, David.

DAVID   I'm not interested in this *crap* anymore.

JEFF   Where's the Maalox? Did you pack the Maalox?

DAVID   Top drawer.

JEFF   It's not *crap.*

DAVID   No?

JEFF   It's maybe *risky.* I can't get the drawer open.

DAVID   Bullshit risky, it's *safe...*

JEFF   *This—?*

DAVID   You said—you have to open this drawer first, *then* that drawer—

JEFF   I opened this fucking drawer...

DAVID   *I* don't know, I hate this goddamn desk. Look, you said, when you brought me Earl's script, when Earl's script was a play, an *interesting* little play being done across the country, "*even in the States.*" You said: This is going to do it for us. This is going to be a brilliant film.

JEFF   That's...

DAVID	And what did I say?
JEFF	You said…
DAVID	I said tone down the sex, tone down the violence, give me *more* about the people, the *people, characters,* their *story,* I said, *that's* where the film is.
JEFF	They're still there.
DAVID	Where? There are no *people* in this screenplay: there's bodies.
JEFF	For fuck's—
DAVID	It's a *slasher* film.
JEFF	That is—
DAVID	What happened to all the *friends,* their re*lat*ionships, and all their *problems* living in the big city, feeling alone, abandoned, unloved? Huh? What happened to that? It's gone, and what have we got? A film about a *serial* killer.
JEFF	That—that is a *slight* oversimplifica—
DAVID	Bites off their nipples, Jeff.
JEFF	So he bites off their nipples…what, are you saying that never happens?
DAVID	Jesus. I'm not interested in making a movie about a guy goes around *raping* women, *slashing* their…
JEFF	Hold on, hold on…
DAVID	Their *tits*…
JEFF	Hold *on*…he does not *rape* them.
DAVID	Oh?
JEFF	He murders th…dumps their bodies in alleyways…

DAVID   Alleyways...

JEFF   Fridges, old boats, it's very...

DAVID   Listen to yourself.

JEFF   It's very inventive, it's current, it's visceral.

DAVID   You should really listen to yourself.

JEFF   *You* should really listen to myself.

DAVID   Okay. Alright. I'll give you "current." I'll give you "inventive." I'll even give you "visceral." Now what I want to know is, and it's a minor detail I know, but what is the fuckin story?

JEFF   Don't pull this shit with—

DAVID   No. What is the story of the film?

JEFF   A group of friends is stalked by a serial killer.

DAVID   *No.* The—you see?—the story. The big story, the story with which an audience—remember them?—can identify, what *is* it?

JEFF   A group of friends—

DAVID   Not the *plot.* Don't tell me the plot. What is the— There are only three stories, Jeff. Right? Right?

JEFF   *Yessss.*

DAVID   The search for faith. The search for redemption. The search for love. Okay. What is the story of Earl's film?

JEFF   The search for love.

DAVID   Wrong. He's taken out the scene with the shrink. Remember, third draft, where he comes to realise his relationships always fail because he fears women, powerful women. Now it's gone. Where did the search for love go, Jeff? It got cut off like the *nipples* of the—

JEFF   The search for redemption, then.

DAVID   He doesn't earn it. The serial killer goes to see the old man, the re*formed* serial killer, and the re*formed* killer says: "Forgive yourself, find it in your heart to forgive." It's a cop-out. For an hour and a half the script tells us there's no forgiveness in this world, and in the last shot an old man says "find it" and this fucker does?

JEFF   Okay. The search for faith.

DAVID   What, his prison conversion to Buddhism? I don't call that a story, I call that a two a.m. rewrite by a hack who's starting to believe his own press. So where is it? Where is the story?

JEFF   Are you telling me you never liked it?

DAVID   You know what I liked about it? When you brought it in? These people, this little circle of friends, they were lost, they had no love, they cheated on each other, they fucked each other, they lied to each other, they couldn't make an honest statement to save their miserable lives, and I thought: alright, something about the world I live in. I understood that these people had no faith; what I *didn't* understand, what Earl *didn't* give me was a way to *live* in this world, to rise *above* the misery. And I said to *you*, I said to *Earl*, I said to anybody who'd listen: this is the heart of the picture, go *deeper* with that, show me how they find the courage to go on living. And what happened? With each draft, Earl took out more and more of the heart and put in more and more of the crap.

JEFF   Give me a week. I can save it.

DAVID   It's beyond saving.

JEFF   He's gonna walk across the street.

DAVID   I got a plane.

JEFF   You are going nowhere 'til we've worked this out.

DAVID   It's worked, and it's out. The project is dead.

JEFF   Listen to me.

DAVID   Sixty-forty. That's it.

JEFF   That's it? You're gonna pull that shit on me? Okay, let's call Jen.

DAVID   Why?

JEFF   'Cause she owns twenty. It's not sixty-forty. It's forty-forty-twenty, and you wanna pull that shit on me, I wanna hear from Jen's twenty.

DAVID   I control Jen's twenty. That's it. I can't make pictures I don't believe in. I have to get back to what I believe in, to where I started, where *we* started. Jeff, in film, in film school, we wanted to make *pictures,* real *films,* with, with heart.

JEFF   Fuck that.

DAVID   With *heart* and, and integrity.

JEFF   I got kids, I can't afford integrity.

DAVID   Come *on. Jeff.*

JEFF   Look, you *change,* your needs change and, *fuck,* you get *ulcers...*

DAVID   You get ulcers one way or the other, you sell out or you don't. I'll take the ulcers with the projects that al*low* me, at the end of the day, to look at myself in the mirror.

JEFF   Well quit looking at the fucking mirror and take a look at the *books,* like *I* do, every *day,* the *books,* which are not *happy.*

DAVID   We're *fine.*

JEFF   No, *you're* Fine. I'm Bloom. The company is *us,* Fine *and* Bloom Pictures. Lest ye have forgotten. And the company is not *happy,* because the company is about to lose a project that could take us to the next *level,* that could make us a player. You know what's gonna happen we don't commit. Talent's not gonna *touch* us. We won a very difficult and very public bidding war for this film, and now you're gonna put it in turnaround because it doesn't meet your your—

DAVID   Stop *talking* like…

JEFF   Your unrealistic notions of—

DAVID   What are you, in Hollywood? "Turnaround," "walk across the." You are sounding more and more like some *hustler,* it's all *talk* with you, it's *attitude, restaurants,* lunch at 990, dinner at North 44. Fuck that. I want to eat in a restaurant that doesn't have a number in its name. What's happening to us? I mean is this really the kind of movie you…Is this the kind of film you want your *children* to know you—What are you lookin…what are you looking at?

JEFF   I could've sworn I saw it…just now…it was all gold and…

DAVID   What?

JEFF   Floatin right above your head, your halo, your bright…

DAVID   Fuck you.

JEFF   You're *pure.*

DAVID   I'm not saying that.

JEFF   *You* didn't greenlight "Meatballs Five". You know as well as I do: the audience dictates what we do. The audience wants *tits,* they get *tits.* You want to give 'em art, we go tits *up.*

DAVID	I'm *gone.*
JEFF	*Go* then. *Go.* Run away, leave it to me to pick up the fuckin pieces.
DAVID	You brought him in.
JEFF	You had *nothing* to do with it. That's right, you're clean, your asshole's *pink.* What do I have to do, beg? Is that what you want? Look. I'll get on the phone with Earl…
DAVID	I don't…
JEFF	*Listen* to me. I'll hold his fuckin hands while he types and break 'em *both* if he doesn't deliver.
DAVID	No…
JEFF	Jesus, give me a *week,* that's all, one week to come up with the—
DAVID	I'm not *interested* in this crap anyMORE.
JEFF	Well would you mind telling me what kinda crap you *are* interested in?
DAVID	It's not crap. You know what kinda movie I wanna make? Read "Zevi".
JEFF	"Zevi", what is that?
DAVID	The script I left on your desk. It is an amaz—it is a brilliant fucking story. It's compelling, it's got great characters, the dialogue is beautiful, it's, it's like poetry.
JEFF	Poetry.
DAVID	I mean, I don't know who this kid is, but she's got a gift, she's got a voice. She knows how to tell a story.
JEFF	What is the story David?

DAVID   It's about the search for faith. It's about a guy, a rabbi...his name is...Sa...Sab...uhh...

JEFF   I'm filled with confidence.

DAVID   Sabbatai Zevi. Okay. 1665. This guy. He'a a rabbi. He announces he's the Messiah, and thousands of Jews, all over Europe, they believe him. They follow him. The movement builds, more Jews join up; then finally, after about a year, he says he's gonna go to Constantinople, take the crown of the Sultan's head, establish the kingdom of Israel. Okay. Now, this is the height of the Ottoman Empire. The Sultan hears Zevi's coming, has him arrested, gives him a choice: prove you're the Messiah, perform a miracle, walk down the street while my archers fire flaming arrows into your body. Do this...or convert to Islam. So he converts. Becomes a Mus—lives the rest of his life as a Muslim. But, even better—the Jews, not all of them, but some of them, *continue to believe*. They think the conversion is part of the *plan*. I mean, isn't that incredible? It's all in here; that basic need we all have when we're feeling lost and hopeless: to find someone who'll give our life meaning.

JEFF   It's a *student film.*

DAVID   It's everything Earl's film should be.

JEFF   *(picking up "Zevi")* It weighs a ton.

DAVID   It's a little long.

JEFF   It's a fuckin murder weapon. *(reading from "Zevi")* Cut to Zevi standing on the hill, his followers all around him. "We are nearing the time of ticken, my children."

DAVID   Tea-koon.

JEFF   Tikkun. Which is what?

DAVID   It's like, mending the world, bringing peace to the world.

JEFF   *"The secrets of kab...kabal..."*

DAVID   Kabbala. Jewish mysticism.

JEFF   Kabbala. This isn't about the search for faith, it's
            about the search for a fucking dictionary.

DAVID   Just read it.

JEFF   *"The time has come for us to go to Constantinople."*
            ...Zevi turns to Nathan.

            Who's Nathan?

DAVID   It's, like his partner.

JEFF   Like his partner. *"I do not know, Nathan, if I will*
            succeed. I only know that I must lead the people, give
            them the divine spark, and bring peace to this"—

            Who the fuck talks like this?

DAVID   Nobody. That's another reason I like it. I'm sick of
            these realistic screenplays, "fuck this, fuck that."

JEFF   *"Sin and sin and sin again ye Jews, for only those who*
            sin may be redeemed."

DAVID   I'm not saying it doesn't need work, it's all over the
            place, she's got *way* too many characters, she's got
            twice the shit she needs in there. But it's a great story,
            Jeff, a *great* story.

            The cell phone rings.

DAVID   Have a little faith, Jeff. You know what I can do with
            a script. I've got a week to—

JEFF   Get the phone.

DAVID   I thought it was you.

JEFF   It's you.

DAVID   *(into phone)* Hello?....*(to JEFF)* Jen....*(into phone)* Hi...I don't...*Jen...*

JEFF   What is it?

DAVID   *(on phone)* Jenny, I can't...Okay. Slow, calm down...Jen, I don't—

JEFF   What's the—

DAVID   Jeff, *please. (on phone)* Jennifer, would ya—*what?* I *can't,* I, you *know*...I've gotta catch my *flight* is why, I've gotta...Look, I'll call you when I get...when I get settled...I'll call middle of the week...don't *do* this. Don't turn this around...Jen...Jenny...*Jennifer—. (hangs up) Fuck's sake.*

JEFF   What?

DAVID   She hung up on me. Did you see that?

JEFF   Why, what was that?

DAVID   I don't know, her fucking cat died. I mean, what'm I supposed to do, cancel my trip for this? I can't go running home everytime she's got some emotional *crisis.*

JEFF   You want me to see her, to...

DAVID   What? *No.* She's my fucking wife, I'll deal with it when I get *back.*

JEFF   Alright.

DAVID   What do you want with her?

JEFF   She's a *friend* for fuck's — *forget* it.

DAVID   I gotta go.

JEFF   *David,* we're not, not *through* here.

DAVID   Look. You came in here, and you said: Make a
               Decision. I've made it. These are the kinds of movies
               we are going to make. I am *this close* to telling this
               girl that I want to make her film.

JEFF   David, if you, if you *think* that we are going to drop
               Earl's script for this Ben Hur shit, you are...

DAVID   I have arrived at the conclusion, Jeff, after years of
               convincing myself that I was living the life I want to
               live, I have arrived at the conclusion that my life is a
               lie. Everything's going to change. My career. My...
               My *desk*. Everything has to change. Earl is dead. Long
               live "Zevi".

3. The Bialik Centre, an old age home, in Toronto.

RACHEL   (*reading from a newspaper*) "Enemies to the death for three decades, Israel and the P.L.O. opened a new era in their blood-soaked history today by recognising each other's legitimacy and the rights of both to represent their people's dreams."

WOLF   Ha. "Dreams."

RACHEL   Should I go on?

WOLF   Go. What else I got to do?

RACHEL   You've got lots.

WOLF   Lox? Where do you see lox?

RACHEL   I said LOTS. You've got LOTS to do.

WOLF   Sure. I could play shuffleboard with Mrs. Blitzstein. You seen the size of her tumour? Like *this.* You know what she does? She *picks* at it. I'm trying to make a shot, and she's picking. Go on. Read.

RACHEL   "In a letter to Prime Minister Yitzha—

WOLF   Don't say that name.

RACHEL   "In a letter to the Prime Minister of Israel, the P.L.O. chairman, Yasser—"

WOLF   And don't say that name either.

RACHEL   Dad: it's a little difficult to read about the peace talks when I can't use the names of—

WOLF   "Peace talks." That's what you think this is?

RACHEL   Uhh…

WOLF   Lies. It's all lies. Words, that's all. If I had a gun...

RACHEL   Dad...

WOLF   If I had a...what am I doing here? I should be there. With a gun. Like I was. In the beginning. I fought for that land. I nearly died for that land. And now? "Here, Arab, take it back." We shoulda got rid of all the Arabs back then. Then we wouldn't be having these talks.

RACHEL   Just...get rid of them.

WOLF   How can you have "peace talks," Rachela? It doesn't make no sense. You either *have* it, or you don't. The day the traitor and the terrorist get on their knees and beg forgiveness of the other, that will be the day there's peace. You know what the Arab wants?

RACHEL   A home?

WOLF   Home schmome. He wants the Jews to say "I'm sorry. I took your land. I murdered your children. I'm sorry. Forgive me." You think we're gonna do that? Why do you tell me these things?

RACHEL   You asked me to read.

WOLF   So make it up.

RACHEL   I'm gonna hit you.

WOLF   Go ahead. Finish me off. At least the last thing I'll see is my beautiful daughter who comes to visit me not like that ungrateful shaygetz-shtupping yenta in Florida. What? You're leaving?

RACHEL   No.

WOLF   You're doing that thing with your leg you do when you want to go.

RACHEL   What thing?

WOLF	Shaking it, shaking your leg.
RACHEL	I'm not shaking my leg.
WOLF	But you have to go.
RACHEL	No, I…
WOLF	Go, who's stopping you?
RACHEL	I don't have to go.
WOLF	What then?
RACHEL	No, I. My plane doesn't leave for a couple of hours.
WOLF	Mm. A whole week this thing?
RACHEL	One week.
WOLF	You're quitting teaching?
RACHEL	I didn't say that.
WOLF	*Films,* what do you want with that?
RACHEL	I. Dad. I. Never mind.
WOLF	You think what you do isn't so important?
RACHEL	Of course it is.
WOLF	It's the most important thing you can do, teaching children. Other than having them.
RACHEL	No.
WOLF	Listen.
RACHEL	I'm not having this conversation.
WOLF	Do me a favour. Mrs. Klein cut from *The Jewish News*…where is it…about a singles dance.

RACHEL   Help me.

WOLF   Out by the airport.

RACHEL   How convenient.

WOLF   All kinds of…

RACHEL   Losers.

WOLF   …Jewish kids…

RACHEL   The hora…the hora…

WOLF   Don't be so stubborn. Honest to God, where do you get it?

RACHEL   I'm 33 and I'm not going to a Jewish singles dance.

WOLF   It isn't right, not to have children

RACHEL   The subject is changing…now.

WOLF   Fine. Get me some herring.

RACHEL   Forget it.

WOLF   In sour cream.

RACHEL   No.

WOLF   It's so much to ask? You walk across the street, there's the Daiter's…

RACHEL   I'm not…

WOLF   A half a tub.

RACHEL   Dad…

WOLF   The lid, I'll give it a lick.

RACHEL   I'm not getting you herring.

WOLF	Fine. It's only the last time I'm gonna see you…
RACHEL	Don't…
WOLF	…I thought maybe you'll do me a little favour…
RACHEL	Jesus, you lay it on, you know that? It sits here, right on my heart.
WOLF	What?
RACHEL	The guilt, Dad. And you know it. You know you're doing it.
WOLF	So gimme credit, I got a talent.
RACHEL	I should go. It's just a week.
WOLF	A lot can happen in a week. A man could die in a week. A people could lose their country in a week.
RACHEL	Another people could get theirs back.
WOLF	I want my country back. I want back the country of the Jews. I don't want to die. Surrounded by old people. In *this* country. This is not my country. I want to go home, Rachela.
RACHEL	I know.
WOLF	I'm going to die. Here. I heard them talking, the doctor and your brother, whispering, they think I couldn't hear them, I could hear them, it's growing in my skull, pressing on my brain, and it's giving me better hearing, taking away my eyes. I'm going to *die*. Alone. In this place.
RACHEL	We all die alone.
WOLF	This is how you comfort me?
RACHEL	You asked me not to lie to you.
WOLF	I want to touch the Western Wall.

RACHEL   You will.

WOLF   No.

RACHEL   You will.

WOLF   Alright. Here. Come here.

> *He puts his hand over her heart, holds it there,*
> *"throws" the guilt away.*

Alright? Now it isn't sitting there.

RACHEL   No.

WOLF   Take me to dinner. Just promise me one thing.

RACHEL   What, Dad.

WOLF   You won't sit me next to the picker.

4. The Writer's Retreat. DAVID's office.

DAVID (*on the phone*) I what?…when did I say…I did not authorise another *draft*…Jeff, I ma…you can fax it, I'm not gonna…I won't read it…I don't give a—

There is a knock at the door.

(*to person at door*) Just a second.

DAVID Jeff don't…*don't*…what?…*what?*…I told you to not to see her…did I not tell you to stay…I don't want to *hear* it…I can't he—I can't *help her*…that is all I'm saying…I am saying goodbye now…I am saying goodbye…goodbye. (*hangs up*)

Come in.

Enter RACHEL.

DAVID Can I help you?

RACHEL I…

DAVID Yes?

RACHEL …have a meeting with…Is this David Fine's office?

DAVID I'm David.

RACHEL Oh. I'm Rachel Benjamin.

DAVID *You're* Rachel Benjamin?

RACHEL Yes. Uhh…aren't we supposed to be…?

DAVID Yes, yes. Absolutely. Yes. Sorry. I just, I don't know what I was…Come in, come in…Have a seat…Well…It's good to *meet* you, finally, in person, finally.

RACHEL Is this a bad time?

DAVID	No, no, it's a good time, it's a perfect time, it's a fine time and I'm fine, are you fine?
RACHEL	I'm fine.
DAVID	Good. Good, we're both fine. Have a, have a seat. Coffee?
RACHEL	Sure.
DAVID	I don't have any. We could go to the lounge.
RACHEL	Uhh...
DAVID	We'll stay here. When'd you get in?
RACHEL	Last night.
DAVID	Been out here before?
RACHEL	Never.
DAVID	Aren't those mountains fantastic?
RACHEL	Oh.
DAVID	How's the compound?
RACHEL	The...?
DAVID	Grounds, have you walked around, or...?
RACHEL	No. I've been in my room, mostly.
DAVID	How is it? Comfortable, comfortable?
RACHEL	It's fine.
DAVID	Need anything?
RACHEL	No, it's. Well...
DAVID	What?

RACHEL   Maybe a softer chair. I screwed up my back couple a years ago.

DAVID   These cutbacks, they're killing us. They used to have nice chairs. I'll order one for you.

RACHEL   No, no.

DAVID   You're gonna be sitting a whole week.

RACHEL   I'll be alright.

DAVID   It's no trouble.

RACHEL   Well, if it's no trouble. My God. I'm turning into my father.

DAVID   Don't fight it. Von day, sho you'll be shpeaking vit an excent you never hed. Oi, oi, I'm heving a Chasid flashback, I, I...so, which dorm you in?

RACHEL   Thompson Hall.

DAVID   Thompson, that's, great, right by the path into town. Room?

RACHEL   212.

DAVID   South side, overlooking the forest.

RACHEL   Yes. It's wonderful, I've got deer outside my window.

DAVID   Deer? You mean elk.

RACHEL   No. Deer. A whole family.

DAVID   Really? I'll have to stop by and...Okay. Um. I just wanted to talk before the, before the group session tomorrow, just to go over some, some things, alright?

RACHEL   Okay.

DAVID   Are you nervous?

RACHEL   No.

DAVID   Good. Good. You seem, but, okay. So.

RACHEL   Are you nervous?

DAVID   Uh. Me? Well. I just had this phone call from, never mind.

RACHEL   Deep breath.

DAVID   Deep breath. Right. Okay, start again. Rachel. I love your script.

RACHEL   Really?

DAVID   You're very talented.

RACHEL   Thank you.

DAVID   I want you to know that. And I want you to keep this moment, right now, right here, in your head. Because there'll be some difficult times, some less than, some, some times when maybe the rewrites won't be working, when the whole thing feels like it's falling apart, when it feels dull, you've looked at the same goddamn scene a hundred times, and it seems dead to you, and you'll think, I wanna give up, you'll think— did you just shower?

RACHEL   Sorry?

DAVID   With some kind of fruit soap or?

RACHEL   Oh. My shampoo. Peach.

DAVID   Peach. Peach shampoo. Okay. All I want to tell you, just now, before we meet, in the group, tomorrow, is, we'll meet tomorrow, and then you're gonna write, and we'll meet in the afternoon to talk, in the group, about how things are going, then we'll all meet for a drink in the lounge, relax, and then more writing, and more writing. Okay?

RACHEL   Do you, uh, think it needs that much work?

DAVID   What?

RACHEL   My script.

DAVID   No. Yes.

RACHEL   Multiple choice?

DAVID   Well. The thing is. It's up to you. I can't tell you what to write. And I won't. I'll tell you what speaks to me, I'll tell you what moves me, but I won't tell you what—or how—to write. You have to find it for yourself, in yourself, or it isn't true. I just want you to know that I'm here for you. "Here for you." What does that mean? Uhh…I do get pompous. Something about the air out here. Umm. Look. You're not what I pictured.

RACHEL   What?

DAVID   Well, you read someone's work, you talk to someone on the phone, you draw up an image and that's, well, but then they're…sitting… and you're talking and…There's something about this screenplay, and I don't know how to define it, that, that…it's the searching quality of it, of your characters. They're looking for something, something to fill this void, this emptiness, in their lives; they're trying to make a connection to, to their spirit, their spirituality. And that search, that attempt to find a connection, is…it's there, it's there, it's just a bit buried, and I want to help you bring it out, by focusing on the story. See, we've forgotten that we're storytellers, first, and that the duty of the storyteller is…what are you doing?

RACHEL   Taking notes.

DAVID   No. No, don't take notes. How can you listen if you take notes?

RACHEL   Right.

DAVID   Uhh, what was I...

RACHEL   The duty of the storyteller.

DAVID   Right. Okay, take notes. The duty of the storyteller is to help us make sense of the world, of our place in the world. Ask yourself what you enjoy when you go to a film, a play, when you read a novel. We crave narrative. We need that, in our lives. We desire sense to be made, because we live in a world that makes less sense every day. Every ideology we grew up with has failed. Nations are breaking up, marriages...No. Here's the thing. We all need someone to give our life purpose. We're all, essentially, we're all alone, we need someone who'll give us love, unconditional love, who'll tell us that who we are is, someone who will validate who we are, you see? Have I lost you?

RACHEL   No. *No.*

DAVID   What is it?

RACHEL   It's crazy.

DAVID   What is? What, what's crazy?

RACHEL   This whole thing. Coming to the retreat, being at the retreat and. To hear someone, to hear *you* talking about my writing in that way, taking it seriously, like it matters.

DAVID   It *does* matter.

RACHEL   I don't know if I'm a writer.

DAVID   Sure you are. It's written all over your script.

RACHEL   I just, to be honest, I wrote it on a dare.

DAVID   A dare.

RACHEL   Bernie, he...

DAVID   Bernie.

RACHEL	Yeah.
DAVID	Your boyfriend husband lover?
RACHEL	My principal.
DAVID	Oh.
RACHEL	He's married.
DAVID	I see. Are you married?
RACHEL	No. Are you?
DAVID	No, I'm...*yeah*, I am.
RACHEL	You are.
DAVID	I don't know why I said...sorry...it's...
RACHEL	I just...It's funny you'd say you're *not*...
DAVID	So Bernie said...
RACHEL	Bernie said. I mean I used to write a lot, all through high school, university but, but, I never had the, what, the drive I guess, to keep going and, I had to make a decision. I became a teacher. Well, the last little while it's been difficult, I've been wondering if I made the right choice and, Bernie's a sort of confidante. I told him I've been wondering did I make the the right choice. This is gonna sound stupid.
DAVID	Say it.
RACHEL	I want to make a difference. You know?
DAVID	I know.
RACHEL	I want to create something that people will see—a lot of people. I want to make them think and feel and question and...
DAVID	So you wrote a screenplay.

RACHEL   So I wrote a screenplay.

DAVID   You started writing poems and you realised…

RACHEL   How did you know?

DAVID   I can tell.

RACHEL   Well. Yes. Then Bernie gave me the brochure for the
                retreat, said how prestigious it is, they only take six
                writers for the film course, it's taught by this respected
                yada yada yada, the whole thing. Then he says, "Write
                a movie, send it in. Do it, or don't talk to me about
                wanting to be a writer again." And here I am,
                wondering what the hell I'm doing here.

DAVID   Well, what you're doing is…Could you lean back a
                little?

RACHEL   Lean—?

DAVID   Into the light. I just. What colour are your eyes?

RACHEL   My—?

DAVID   Are they green or what?

RACHEL   Sometimes they're green. Sometimes they're grey.
                Depends on the light.

DAVID   Right. Depends on the—Did you eat?

RACHEL   What?

DAVID   Lunch.

RACHEL   No, no, I was too nervous, I couldn't eat.

DAVID   Well. Are you nervous now?

RACHEL   A little. Are you?

DAVID   Oh yes. Very. Why don't we go into town.

RACHEL	Town?
DAVID	There's a path through the forest. Drop off your stuff, hop on a couple of elk—or deer—head down to, I mean, if you, no, forget it.
RACHEL	No. Dinner?
DAVID	No. No. I'm sorry. I shouldn't…
RACHEL	No, it's just, I have to make a phone call and…
DAVID	And?
RACHEL	I mean you're married. Aren't you?
DAVID	Yes. Yes I am.
RACHEL	I'm not saying I wouldn't be interested in, in having dinner if…
DAVID	No, no.
RACHEL	If it was just…
DAVID	That's all it is.
RACHEL	Then.
DAVID	Then let's go.
RACHEL	Right now?
DAVID	No. Tomorrow.
RACHEL	Yes.
DAVID	There's a wonderful noodle house…Japanese noodles…do you eat Japanese noodles?…Rachel.
RACHEL	Sure.
DAVID	Good. Good. Well. I think that's enough for now.
RACHEL	Oh. I agree. I think that's plenty.

5. *The Bialik Centre.*

WOLF *(on phone)* Listen, you got two people who don't trust each other...that's right...that's what it comes down to...oh...oh ho ho ho, so they can sit across all the tables they want, they can shake their hands and make their speeches, it don't matter, because there's no trust, and there won't never be peace, and that's that...believe what you want, Rachela. What do I know? I'm only an old man. Go on, read...what?...so late you're eating?...oh, I forgot...so where you going?...ooh, pish pish pish...with who?...with who?...really...is he single?...alright so I can ask...he's Jewish, that I know...what else makes movies?...so?...don't be silly: how can I be anti-myself?...so, you didn't answer: is he single?...uh huh...and you're having dinner with him...did I say? I didn't say. I did not, I gotta say it: Be careful. Please...Yeah, yeah, it's only dinner. "Ah kashe oif ah frageh." You know what that means? ...Never mind...Alright, go. Have a good time...So when'll I see you?...not before?...okay. No, it's just. It's nice to see your face, that's all...alright...Have a good time...Goodnight.

6. *The forest.*

DAVID   What'd did you think? Of the session, this morning?

RACHEL   Well. I felt a little…

DAVID   Uh huh.

RACHEL   Uncomfortable.

DAVID   Really…did I—was it me?

RACHEL   No no, you made it, it was very relaxed, jokey, it was, no, not that. Is that a graveyard?

DAVID   Uh huh. What is it, what made you…

RACHEL   It's me, I don't know, everyone else is so, *con*fident. It's beautiful in here.

DAVID   Are you kidding? They're scared to death, just like you. They want to hear how good they are.

RACHEL   And you tell them?

DAVID   What's the use in pointing out flaws? It's easy to destroy someone—just find their weakness. Listen, I know this novelist, well respected, wins awards— watch the elk shit—he brings out a book, gets five good reviews and one bad one, which one does he remember?

RACHEL   The bad one obviously.

DAVID   Exactly. Because it confirms his belief that he's basically a fraud; which he's not. And neither are you. Of course you're nervous; it's you, it's you on the page. So, someone comes along and says—what a piece of crap—what are they saying? You're a piece of crap. It happens. It's gonna happen. I mean, it kills me: we spend half our time making art about the absence of, what, love, trust, sympathy, and the other

half the time we sit around cutting our friends lives
and work to shreds. The point is, you have to—what?

RACHEL   Would that be an elk?

DAVID   Ohhhh my goodness yes. A large elk. I don't think she
likes us. Come on, there's another trail up here. We'll
go around.

She stretches her arms above her head.

DAVID   Wh—what are you doing?

RACHEL   Makes 'em think you're an elk.

DAVID   Are you insane? Do, do you know what one of those
things can—a woman was nearly killed here two years
ago, don't, don't be a hero, come on.

She walks toward the elk, shouting "Ha! ha!"

DAVID   Rachel? Rachel!

He follows, attempting to imitate her.

7. *The restaurant.*

DAVID   I can't believe you.

RACHEL   What, it was in the handbook.

DAVID   Jesus, I've never seen that.

RACHEL   It worked, didn't it?

DAVID   Yeah, but…hey.

RACHEL   What?

DAVID   I thought I ordered the tempura.

RACHEL   You did.

DAVID   I know but, this is with the platter.

RACHEL   So?

DAVID   I didn't want the platter, I wanted the á la carte.

RACHEL   Well that's what you got.

DAVID   I did?

RACHEL   Yeah.

DAVID   Great. Tell me about the poems.

RACHEL   Hm?

DAVID   You were gonna tell me about how you started writing poems and they turned into a screenplay. I'm a very good listener.

RACHEL   You really want to hear this?

DAVID   You really want to tell me?

RACHEL   You are *so* Jewish.

DAVID   What do you mean?

RACHEL   Nothing. Alright. I was writing these poems, as Zevi. He was talking about how the world is broken, how we have to fix the world, by committing acts of tikkun, repenting for our sins. Then one day, I don't know how, it just happened, I had him talking to Nathan, the prophet. Then these two guys, they just...

DAVID   They took over.

RACHEL   Yes.

DAVID   You couldn't get them out of your head.

RACHEL   *Yes.* They, they *insisted* on being heard.

DAVID   Uh huh uh huh.

RACHEL   Then I saw "The Last Temptation of Christ".

DAVID   Brilliant film.

RACHEL   *Brilliant* film.

DAVID   He pulls out his heart.

RACHEL   Oh my *God.*

DAVID   The music.

RACHEL   Isn't it?

DAVID   I don't know about these guys with the Brooklyn accents—but whatever, whatever, it was a movie about a *man* struggling with, with—

RACHEL   With his demons, David.

DAVID   Exactly, his *demons, yes.*

RACHEL   And I thought, *I* want to do that, I *wish* I could do that but...

DAVID   Wine?

RACHEL   Yeah...but I don't want to just focus on the leader, I want to know about the people...

DAVID   Right.

RACHEL   ...the followers. Am I boring you?

DAVID   *Boring* me?

RACHEL   You must get this all the time.

DAVID   *I* asked *you.* Go on.

RACHEL   I started to see it, as a movie.

DAVID   The Last Tempura of, sorry. You started to see it as a movie, yes.

RACHEL   But I wasn't sure, I didn't know what it *meant, why* I was writing the—

DAVID   That's what writing is, the discovery. *You* discover it, *we* discover it.

RACHEL   Okay. But—I didn't know how it was relevant, to my life, to other peoples lives. Then this one day, I'm sitting there, talking to my Dad...

DAVID   Yeah, your Dad.

RACHEL   Sorry, went off for a minute.

DAVID   Welcome back. We're talking with Rachel Benjamin about her movie, "Zevi".

RACHEL   He's at the Bialik. Brain tumour.

DAVID   Oh...jeez, I'm sorry, I—

RACHEL   No, no, he's *dying,* it's…a fact, you face it, why
           pretend? I see him almost every day. We sit, we talk,
           we argue. It's funny. In a way, he's more alive to me
           now than…You know, you have this way of looking
           at a person.

DAVID   Me? H—what way?

RACHEL   …Dad starts telling me about his life in Israel. He'd
           never talked about it before. Suddenly I'm sitting
           eating herring in sour cream from Daiter's listening to
           stories about how when he was fifteen the Nazis came,
           he escapes to the forest with his two sisters and a
           brother—I mean, this is incredible, can you
           imagine?—meets Begin.

DAVID   Really…

RACHEL   Goes to Israel, he's one of the Betar Boys. I mean, my
           father was a terrorist.

DAVID   There's your tv series.

RACHEL   I know, it's totally unbelievable.

DAVID   What'd he do, like blow up buses?

RACHEL   Close. Train tracks. That was his specialty. And this
           is when things started to connect for me. Here's this
           boy who's lost his parents, his whole world, he's got
           nothing, no hope. Then he meets this messiah, okay?,
           key word, who says, and this is how my Dad talks
           about it, "follow me to Israel to build the land of the
           Jews", right, a land of freedom from murder and
           oppression—but, David, what does this new world
           become but a land of murder and oppression. And
           people like my father, they become disillusioned, they
           feel betrayed, they leave, they long to return. And I
           started thinking, of course: the Zionist leaders are just
           like Zevi, and the Holocaust survivors are like his
           followers. It's the same story, of despair, followed by
           a vision of…what?

DAVID   Nothing.

RACHEL   You disagree? Don't tell me you're a Zionist.

DAVID   No, I. I don't follow Israel.

RACHEL   Really?

DAVID   Really.

RACHEL   You're a Jew.

DAVID   Jew...ish. I mean: don't get me wrong, your father's story is terrific, but, what does it have to with your screenplay?

RACHEL   That's what this movie's a*bout.*

DAVID   Your screenplay.

RACHEL   Yes.

DAVID   Is about...

RACHEL   Israel.

DAVID   I don't see it. I don't get that. Explain that to me.

RACHEL   Well...

DAVID   I mean, you've written a beautiful screenplay about *a man,* the, the *inner* life, his *struggle.* This stuff about Israel, it's, I mean...

RACHEL   Are you saying forget about Israel?

DAVID   No, I. It's up to you. All I'm saying is, don't force it to become *about* something, especially something as ephemeral as, as, a political struggle, *especially* when what it *really* wants to be about is. Look. Let me give you an example of what I'm talking about. This is how I work. I *respond.* And if you trust me, my instincts, you'll write more of what *speaks* to—That's how it comes out. This speech of Zevi, where is it, I marked it, the speech to his wife.

RACHEL	Sarah.
DAVID	I love this. Can I read it? Do you mind?
RACHEL	Here?
DAVID	I'll keep it quiet. "Sarah, my love, there is one great love. Only one. In one's lifetime. And we must find it. Or we will be lost, all our lives. Though we share a bed, you are not my great love. My great love is Torah. Only through Her do I feel alive. Only though Her do I live. I must leave you Sarah, for Torah."
	That's wonderful. The courage of the man. To leave his...It's.
RACHEL	Were you an actor?
DAVID	What? Oh, years ago. I left it. Why?
RACHEL	I thought you read really well.
DAVID	Come on. You thought I read that well?
RACHEL	What I heard, yeah.
DAVID	What you heard?
RACHEL	It was...hard to...Why did you stop?
DAVID	Well, that's the...end of the speech...
RACHEL	Acting. Why did you stop acting?
DAVID	Oh...well. I went to film school.
RACHEL	To act?
DAVID	No. No, to...write. But. I didn't have the, I don't know, I guess I didn't have the one thing successful artists have: courage. To believe I could do it. That what I wrote *mattered*. And I didn't exactly have anyone *telling* me it mattered. Well, Jeff.

RACHEL   Jeff? Your boyfriend husband lover?

DAVID   My partner. Jeff Bloom. We got together, he said he
wanted to produce my screenplay. That's all he wanted
to do: be a movie producer, from Day One. But. I just.
I didn't have the *confidence.* We ended doing another
film, amazing, it won awards, it was shown on
television. Then we got into distribution. We just kept
going. It takes over, the producing stuff. You start
living this life you never really wanted, why, because
it's comfortable, it's safe, you don't ask yourself why
you do the things you do, you just do them. It takes
you over, and you don't even know it's happening, and
that's the. One day, Jeff comes into my office, hands
me a script, tells me he's found it in a drawer, I oughta
give it a read. It was about a man who wanted to be
Good, to do Good. But he couldn't. He could *see* it: he
just couldn't do it. So he sits in his room, recalling
his life, trying to pinpoint the place where he stopped
being good. It was naive but. I actually sat there
weeping over this thing. The cover'd been torn off, and
when I asked Jeff who wrote it, he said, "You did,
David." It was the script I wrote back in school. He
thought I'd enjoy it. Thought I'd Get A Kick Out Of
It. Fifteen years of being a producer, a hustler, money
man, I'd gone so far away from being an artist, I
couldn't even recognise the artist in myself. I couldn't
recognise myself. Rachel. Right now. I look at you,
and I see in you what I wanted to be. I can see, I can
see you need someone to help you find the courage
to…Rachel do this. Right now. Say this: " I am a
writer."

RACHEL   Come on.

DAVID   I mean it.

RACHEL   No.

DAVID   You say it right now or I'm leaving. I'm not gonna
waste my time on someone who doesn't believe in
herself. You got three seconds. One. Two.

RACHEL   I…am…

DAVID   See ya.

He gets up.

RACHEL   I'm a writer.

DAVID   Take your hands away.

RACHEL   I'm a writer.

DAVID   Can't hear you.

RACHEL   I'M A WRITER. I AM A WRITER. *I AM A WRITER.*

He sits.

DAVID   You write only what you believe. Only that. Not what I want. Not what the audience wants. Not what the investors, the granting agencies, the critics, the, you commit yourself to the story, you sacrifice everything to that story and never betray it. That is your duty, and if you give it up, you'll end up like me. Maybe you'll have success. But you'll have regrets. All your life, you'll have regrets...

RACHEL   Do you really like it?

DAVID   What?

RACHEL   My screenplay.

DAVID   Rachel. I. I'm gonna shock you a little. I've been going though a sort of crisis, lately, well, on a couple of fronts, and...never mind...on the creative front...I've been uninspired by the sort of *stuff* that crosses my desk and...when I read your screenplay, I...it brought me back to a place that, when I started making movies...see, this is all I have now, making other people's movies, and I *won't,* I will not let...

The point is I've made a decision, an impor...

JEFF   *(off)* IT'S OKAY, I SEE HIM.

DAVID   …No.

RACHEL   What?

DAVID   I don't believe it.

JEFF   *(entering)* David! They said you'd be here and here you
         are and here I am and here are the rewrites. *Here are the
         rewrites,* made to order, David, made to fucking *order.*

DAVID   What. Are you doing?

JEFF   Read 'em and weep, pal, read 'em and—

DAVID   I'm in the *middle* of—

JEFF   You're in the middle of nowhere, I don't mind
         telling— *Oh.* I'm sorry.

RACHEL   Hello.

JEFF   Jeff Bloom.

RACHEL   Oh, David's…

JEFF   Partner, and you are?

RACHEL   Rachel Benjamin.

JEFF   *The* Rachel Ben—The Rachel Benjamin this son-of-a-
         bitch can't stop *raving* about?

DAVID   Jeff, this isn't the—

JEFF   What are you, having a story meeting or something?

RACHEL   We're just…

JEFF   Script's on the table, that's what gave me the idea.

DAVID   Yes, we're having a story meeting. This is a writer's
         retreat.

JEFF	Sound the alarm! Retreat! Sorry, I just flew Toronto-Calgary on not much sleep, I'm wired, wired, does it show or do I just seem my usual fast-talking Jew self? Never mind, trick question, how would you know, Jew know, get it, Jew know, I love that Woody Allen, shove over, what is this? Tempura? No thanks, I ate on the plane. Hey, Rachel, David, I'm sorry, I don't mean to interrupt, I was hoping to catch you up the hill there up at the uhh the uhh campus or whatever, and I'm looking I'm looking all over for you, somebody tells me you've gone to town, some noodle place, they didn't know, there's a hundred of 'em, just go have a look. So I'm in the Jimmy, you ever driven one of these things, I'm getting one the minute I get back to T.O., and I come round this corner and *boom* outta the bush comes this freight train of an elk. I'm not kidding. Huge—
DAVID	Is this a long story?
JEFF	You still here? Look, you gonna read these rewrites or what?
DAVID	"What."
RACHEL	I can leave if you guys need to talk or…
DAVID	We don't need to talk.
JEFF	Rachel, I'm sorry. I, it's just, we have some very important business to conduct. Fine-Bloom Pictures is on the verge of a major deal.
RACHEL	Really.
JEFF	He didn't tell you? He's so modest. We're about to commit to the hottest property in the country, aren't we, David?
DAVID	No.

JEFF	See, we're trying to run a business, only David here keeps running away, always running away from his problems. David. Take the rewrites. Go sit in the john and read 'em. I mean it.
DAVID	I told you…
JEFF	Well then as long as we're sitting here talking story ideas why don't we talk about Lake Charlotte? This your wine, David?
RACHEL	Would you like a glass?
JEFF	That's okay, we share everything. Speaking of which, Lake Charlotte.
DAVID	I don't think this is really…
JEFF	Lake Charlotte, Rachel, is a film project that David and I have been developing for years, years. Would you like to hear about Lake Charlotte?
DAVID	No, she wouldn't.
JEFF	Okay. It's about these two old friends, two men, and the fiancee of one of the men. They're all very close. In fact, they created this little business together. Well, to celebrate the growing success of this little business, the three of them go off on this little vacation.
DAVID	I hate this story.
JEFF	It's not a story, it's a plot. It's about the search for love.
DAVID	Give me the rewrites.
JEFF	No, no, I don't want to interrupt…
DAVID	Give. Me. The rewrites. Rachel. I'm sorry. I won't be long.
JEFF	Sure you will. Off you go. Men's room. Down the hall, turn left.

Exit DAVID. They sit there a moment.

JEFF   You enjoy working with David?

RACHEL   What?

JEFF   On the script I mean.

RACHEL   Yeah he's great, he's…

JEFF   You're very lucky. *Very* lucky, to have the best story editor in the country. You know Paramount wanted him?

RACHEL   Paramount *Pictures?*

JEFF   Yyyyyes. But Jen didn't want to go to L.A.

RACHEL   Jen.

JEFF   His wife. Did he tell you he was married?

RACHEL   Yes.

JEFF   Hm. Anyway, they all want him, the guy's an alchemist with scripts. And I gotta tell you, when he shoved your script in my face I said, "Are you kidding? Like I've got time to read some student script when I'm up to here in negotiations with Keanu's agent?"

RACHEL   Keanu Reeves?

JEFF   Uh huh.

RACHEL   Is gonna be in your next movie?

JEFF   Keanu and, cross your fingers, Winona. Right now, Miramax *and* Goldwyn are fighting over U.S. distribution. I got Channel Four on one line, Canal Plus on—oh excuse me, Canal Pleu—on the other—I mean, this thing is huge. So you can see why I was a little hestitant to pick up your script. But, I had some time to kill on the plane, so I read it. Do you know where Quail Avenue is?

RACHEL	Quail?
JEFF	Something like that. All the streets around here, they're named for animals. Yeah, Quail Avenue.
RACHEL	I think it's to the left. Um. What did you think?
JEFF	Of?
RACHEL	My script?
JEFF	I better not say.
RACHEL	Why not?
JEFF	This is David's thing.
RACHEL	No, it's my thing. I wrote it.
JEFF	And David's helping you rewrite it. Look, he's got his way of working, I got mine. See, David thinks it's his job to make you feel good.
RACHEL	He says a writer needs unconditional love.
JEFF	Exactly. He thinks it's theoretically possible that a writer who gets patted on the...back will produce a better script. Now, I take a more practical approach. See, it's all very nice coming out here to this artist's retreat and climbing mountains and doo-dah doo-dah, but in the real world, you got to do the work. Look. Mountain climbing. An amateur does it for fun. There's a trail, you follow the trail. That's not mountain climbing. A real mountain climber, he's got the belt and the hooks and the ropes and the this and the, there's a craft, and if you're serious, you go out, you get the tools, you *learn how to climb*. And that is what you should be doing if you want to make it in this business. Now, this is not the worst thing I've ever read. It's got possibilities. You take it to any producer in the real world, he's gonna tell you the same thing: it needs work.
RACHEL	A lot of work?

JEFF	Look. I don't want to screw you up.
RACHEL	I'm asking you.
JEFF	And I'm telling you, stick with David, you'll be fine.
RACHEL	I don't want to be fine, I want to...bloom.
JEFF	Oh, that's good.
RACHEL	Just, tell me what you think.
JEFF	You don't give up, do ya?
RACHEL	I'm tenacious.
JEFF	I'm...I wouldn't feel comfortable.
RACHEL	I won't tell David if you won't.
JEFF	Alright. Lemme ask you: did you work from an outline?
RACHEL	Outline?
JEFF	I didn't think so. You write it as a story first. Thing is, you can't write a good screenplay without a good outline. And you can't write a good outline 'til you've figured out the premise. I mean, a solid premise, the who does what to whom premise, which tells you in a sentence whose story it is. Once you've done that, you do your character work. Who are they? Where do they come from? Who were their parents? What do they like? What do they fear? What do they want the most. That's the key. Because you get one guy who wants this, the other one wants that, you draw lines, and where those lines intersect, hello, conflict. Then figure out your plots, your A plot, your B plot, your C plot.
RACHEL	That's a lot of plotzing.

JEFF	I'll do the jokes. Next, break it down into beats, put the beats on cards, pin the cards to your wall, break it down, do the drill. Then, what is it you want to say? The theme? The message? Once you've done that, your premise, your characters, your plot, your theme, the rest is easy. The dialogue is a piece of cake. Remember, your characters are puppets. They say what you want them to say. Are you tracking with this?
RACHEL	It all seems...
JEFF	I know what it seems, but, believe me, you do the work, you're gonna have something to show for it. Okay. Specifics. Why do the Jews believe in Zevi?
RACHEL	Well...the Cossacks...
JEFF	Uh huh?
RACHEL	Nathan talks about them in that scene in the cave.
JEFF	Remind me.
RACHEL	About fifteen years before—
JEFF	This is back story?
RACHEL	What?
JEFF	This happens before the movie starts.
RACHEL	Yes. In 1648, there had been a massacre in...
JEFF	Speak in the present tense. It's happening *now*.
RACHEL	In 1648, there's a pogrom in Poland, the Cossacks...murder hundreds of thousands of Jews, massacre babies, rape women, cut open their bellies and sew live cats inside, and the Jews of—
JEFF	Really?
RACHEL	Yes—

JEFF   Live cats…

RACHEL   —the Jews, who've been living in ghettos, who've been oppressed…

JEFF   Ghettos…

RACHEL   —they've already turned to Kabbala.

JEFF   Mysticism.

RACHEL   That's right, because traditional Jewish teachings didn't have the answers, the rabbis didn't have the answers, couldn't say, Your misery will end when… whereas the Kabbalists constructed this elaborate system that allowed for a direct connection between man and God. Like, the words in the Torah should be understood as numbers, and if you understand the code, you can touch God, you can experience God, they believed you could take the Hebrew letters for God and say them every whch way until you finally *hit* the *real* name and could *see* him. The Kabbala explains the Jewish exile in cosmic terms, but also contains a practical way to return to Israel, by committing acts of tikkun. And when we've all done our tikkun, the world will be mended, the Messiah will come and lead us into Israel. So, in a way, the Jews were, are, prepared to believe in Zevi. Is that, does that…?

JEFF   Well. Intellectually, I understand all that. And, honest to God, if you're my Comparative Religion professor, I'm sitting here entranced. But, come on, we're making a movie here. You've got to make this more…visceral. We've got to feel it. Now what if…it's just an idea, I'm just taking your premise and playing around with it and making suggestions which you can take or reject…

RACHEL   No, no…

JEFF   Okay?…what if as a kind of prelude, a first scene, we go back to this Cossack thing, show the horror of it, take me into the ghettos, show me the raping and the killing, the business with the live cats…it's horrifying, yes, but it will *help us understand* where the Jews *are*. They've been decimated, they have no hope, maybe an old man looks up and cries out "Why have you forsaken us?" something like that, find your own words, and then a Cossack slashes his throat...*Then*, cut to Zevi, this, this *visionary,* doing his Messiah thing, you know, that terrific speech where he says "The time has come to go to Constantinople". Next cut: show me the faces of the Jews, the young, the old, the tired, the hungry, listening, drinking it in. We *need* to see them being *moved*. Film is not about words. It's about images. It's a story told in pictures with a beginning, a middle and an end, and it's told in *cuts*. What do you think?

RACHEL   I...I just...I don't think that's the direction David wants me to go.

JEFF   Oh? What direction does David want you to go?

RACHEL   Well I'm. Not sure.

JEFF   Exactly. Look. You got, what, a week? You want results, you gotta do the work. So. You tell me. I'm more than happy to sit here, go through the whole damn thing with you. For example, the Nathan character.

RACHEL   Yes?

JEFF   Very intriguing. I don't think there's enough about him.

RACHEL   He's in almost every scene.

JEFF   I know, and it's fantastic. I mean, I love that bit where Zevi confides in him about his fears of failure. It just makes me want to know more about him. In fact, I want to know more about *all* of them. What about the wife?

RACHEL   Sarah.

JEFF   Yeah. What's she like? I mean, really like. Because, to
                    be honest, I find it surprising that you, a woman,
                    could *write* a woman who's so easily *duped.*.

RACHEL   Duped?

JEFF   She gets taken in by Zevi. He strings her along, the
                    whole time. I mean, let's face it. Zevi's in love with
                    the Torah, right?

RACHEL   Yes.

JEFF   He's married to Sarah and he leaves her for the Torah.

RACHEL   He makes love to the Torah.

JEFF   Exactly, he—say that again?

RACHEL   He makes *love* to the Torah. They talk about it at the
                    graveyard, the rabbis...

JEFF   He actually — you'll pardon the expression — *fucks* a
                    Torah?

RACHEL   It's just a rumour.

JEFF   *Rumour?* Forget rumour, that's *priceless* that shit.
                    Show me that. It's brilliant: Zevi fucks Torahs. Sarah
                    feels abandoned. Enter Nathan. So to speak.

RACHEL   Sarah's a spiritual w...what do you mean, "enter
                    Nathan."

JEFF   What if Nathan's in love with Sarah?

RACHEL   Why?

JEFF   It's possible, isn't it? Alright: love, that's too strong,
                    we throw it around, "I loved your performance," "I
                    loved the lighting," "I loved your script," but: what if
                    Nathan sleeps with Sarah?

RACHEL   Well...

JEFF	People fucked back then, didn't they?
RACHEL	Of course.
JEFF	So while Zevi is diddling the Torah, isn't it possible that Nathan might be bid-a-boom-bid-a-bang with Sarah?
RACHEL	No.
JEFF	Why not?
RACHEL	Well.
JEFF	Think about this. Close-up on Zevi. Says something like, "Oh, my love. The time has come. The time has come for us to be together, at last, at long last." Right? Now, long shot, Zevi is standing by his bed. On the bed is a Torah scroll. N—just listen. He's naked. Gets in the bed. Caresses the Torah, removes its covering, like he's undressing it, huh? You tracking with this?
RACHEL	I...
JEFF	It's just an idea. He separates the scrolls, as though spreading its legs. He kisses it, up and down. Cut to Nathan and Sarah, in Nathan's house, kissing, caressing. They fall to the floor. Back to Zevi, now straddling the Torah, fucking it, calling the name of God. Cut back to Nathan and Sarah. They're also fucking, calling each other's names. Back to Zevi. He comes, falls forward. Back to the lovers. Nathan comes, falls forward into Sarah's arms. They lie there. Fade. Something like that.
RACHEL	Sarah would never do that.
JEFF	Sure she would.
RACHEL	It's my movie.
JEFF	Then you should know. It makes her...

RACHEL	What?
JEFF	More human, don't you think?
RACHEL	More human.
JEFF	What do you think?
RACHEL	What if…
JEFF	Go for it.
RACHEL	What if Zevi finds out that Sarah and Nathan…made love and…that's what makes him choose, finally, between Sarah and Torah?
JEFF	Yes.
RACHEL	His one great love.
JEFF	"His one great love."
RACHEL	It's stupid isn't it?
JEFF	No. *No.* It's very real. Very human.The search for love. That's the story. *That's* the story you have to tell.

8. RACHEL's room. Enter DAVID.

RACHEL   David?

DAVID   Sorry. It was open. What happened? Where'd you go?

RACHEL   I...

DAVID   I came out of the bathroom, you were gone.

RACHEL   Well, Jeff said you'd be a while and...

DAVID   And...

RACHEL   I wanted to get to work.

DAVID   Good. You get inspired?

RACHEL   Yeah.

DAVID   Can I uhh...

RACHEL   Can you what.

DAVID   Have a look?

RACHEL   No.

DAVID   No. You're right. Good. Well. Goodnight. No. There's something I want to tell you... Um....Well, I should let you work. *(he starts to go)*

RACHEL   Did you read the...

DAVID   Huh?

RACHEL   Screenplay?

DAVID   What?

RACHEL   The screenplay Jeff gave you.

DAVID   Oh. Yeah.

RACHEL   How is it?

DAVID   Crap. Who cares? Rachel.

RACHEL   What?

DAVID   Nothing.

RACHEL   Are you okay?

DAVID   Oh. I'm... *(sees chart)* What's this?

RACHEL   The sefiroth.

DAVID   Ah.

RACHEL   The emanations of God.

DAVID   Right. Um. Right.

RACHEL   Look. Can you read Hebrew?

DAVID   Yeah, but only left to right, so...

RACHEL   Where's my...I had a pen...

DAVID   This it?

RACHEL   Thanks. *(she grabs it; he doesn't let go)* David?

DAVID   Sorry.

RACHEL   When God retracted to make room for the creation, he
            left a streak of light. The light formed itself into
            these...ten vessels...the ten emanations, which
            arranged themselves in the shape of a man, of Adam.
            This is the head *(writing)* Keter.

DAVID   Keter.

RACHEL   And uh, these are the feet, Shechinah.

DAVID   Shekinah.

RACHEL   Ch...She*chi*nah.

DAVID   Shekinah.

RACHEL   We'll work on it. Now out of the eyes
of...Adam...came a light, which...shattered the lower
vessels.

DAVID   Mm hm.

RACHEL   Out of the vessels fells...sparks of...light. You um...

DAVID   Mm?

RACHEL   Have a...

DAVID   What?

RACHEL   An eyelash. *(wipes it away)* Um.

DAVID   Sparks, you were, talking about...

RACHEL   Sparks. Well. The sparks became trapped by evil.
Nathan said that each spark was a Jewish soul. In
exile. And that the way to restore the...um...

DAVID   Light?

RACHEL   The...what?

DAVID   The only way to restore the light...

RACHEL   Yes. To end our time in exile...is to commit tikkun.

DAVID   The mending.

RACHEL   That's right. But um. The trick. The trick is to
know...exactly what your soul needs...in order to be...

          They kiss.

RACHEL   O. Kay.

DAVID	Okay?
RACHEL	Go stand in the corner.
DAVID	Rachel.
RACHEL	Go on. Stand in the corner.

He does.

RACHEL	We have to talk.
DAVID	I hate this part.
RACHEL	You do this a lot?
DAVID	No.
RACHEL	Then why did you say.
DAVID	It's just talk, I'm nervous.
RACHEL	What did Jeff mean, in the restaurant, about ...
DAVID	What?
RACHEL	He asked if I knew you were married, and when I said I did, he said—
DAVID	It didn't mean anything, he just likes to talk.
RACHEL	You guys like to talk.
DAVID	Look. I've been married fifteen years. I'm not a saint. I've...yes...once or twice, I've...*once or twice* in fifteen years, is that so...?
RACHEL	It's not for me to say.
DAVID	Look.
RACHEL	You're married.
DAVID	It's over.

RACHEL	No, no, no.
DAVID	I'm telling you.
RACHEL	Are you divorced?
DAVID	No.
RACHEL	Separated?
DAVID	Not, no.
RACHEL	Living together?
DAVID	We, yes.
RACHEL	Sleeping together.
DAVID	We sleep in the same bed...
RACHEL	Do you fuck?
DAVID	We...sure...
RACHEL	That's a pretty wide definition of "it's over."
DAVID	It *is* over. It's just...convenient...right now...for me to be...living...Look. Rachel. I can't...*stop*...
RACHEL	Don't.
DAVID	I can't stop thinking about you.
RACHEL	Don't do this.
DAVID	When you walked in, into my office, I mean, you think, why do you think, I could hardly speak...at first, I mean...you...you're absolutely...
RACHEL	That's *it*. I mean it. Don't say anything.
DAVID	But I.

RACHEL   Nothing. Let *me* say something. I want to be *clear*. I. Will. Not. Get. Involved. With a married man. Is that clear?

DAVID   But I.

RACHEL   That's it. Stop looking at me like that.

DAVID   Like what?

RACHEL   Like those deer.

DAVID   Alright. I want to see these deer.

RACHEL   Stay in that corner. David, stay...stay in that... *(he goes to her and they kiss)* I will not get. Involved. *(they kiss)* With a married. *(they kiss)* It isn't right. It isn't right.

DAVID   What's your point?

RACHEL   My point? My point is. Lock the door.

ACT TWO

9. Top of a mountain.

RACHEL   *(off)* David, don't!

DAVID   *(off)* Don't what?

RACHEL   *(off)* Throw it down. Throw that snow down, David. I mean it.

DAVID   *(off)* Alright, alright, it's down.

RACHEL   *(screams off)* Liar!

RACHEL runs on, followed by DAVID. He catches her.

DAVID   Alright, my pretty...

RACHEL   David don't...

DAVID   Where are those rewrites?

RACHEL   No! Not down my back! I hate snow down my back please don't please don't...

DAVID   You gonna let me see the rewites?

RACHEL   No!

DAVID   Here it comes!

RACHEL   Alrightalrightalrightalright I'll let you see them I'll let you see them don't throw that snow down MY BACK.

DAVID   *(shows he has no snow)* What snow? I don't have any snow, what are you screaming about?

RACHEL   No snow?

DAVID   No snow.

RACHEL   No rewrites.

DAVID   I'll get some snow.

RACHEL   *No*. They're not *ready*.

DAVID   It's Thursday.

RACHEL   I know. But you said we could work at our own pace.

DAVID   We leave Sunday. That gives you...

RACHEL   "Show me stuff when you feel it's ready to be shown."

DAVID   Yyyeah, it's just.

RACHEL   It's just what?

DAVID   Okay. No pressure. Let's just...okay?

RACHEL   Okay.

DAVID   It's beautiful out here. Listen to that. Silence. This is my favourite spot. You can see everything. There's the town, see?

RACHEL   At the edge of the forest?

DAVID   That's where we walked down.

RACHEL   I love your hair.

DAVID   This is what I want. This is why I come here. You see the water cutting through the rock, and, and you hear it, the rush of it and you think, it's been here millions of years. It was here before I was born, it'll be here after I'm gone. How does that make you feel?

RACHEL   Like jumping in.

DAVID   It shouldn't. It should remind you of. It should give you a reason to keep going. Because it is beautiful. Because you can hear the water rushing. And we're standing here. That's all there is in the world. The phone isn't ringing. You're not stuck in traffic, or reading the paper, or worried about your health or. Everything seems so insignificant, and in that insignificance, all the worries and fears vanish. There's nothing to be afraid of.

RACHEL   What are you afraid of, David?...What's so funny?

DAVID   Nothing. Nothing.

RACHEL   You know. Standing here? It makes me think about...the followers, they, they encamped on a mountain, you know? And. It would have been just them, just, out here, and the sky and them and, you can understand, you can really understand how they could believe in the Kabbala, in Zevi. They, they thought the world started when God retracted. Like, in the beginning, there was only God, and he was lonely. So he gave up a piece of himself to create the world. To create us. He loved us. Then of course we fucked everything up, by not loving him back, not loving each other, being afraid of each other. But I love that idea that you have to give up a piece of yourself in order to love, I mean, to really love.

           He puts his arm around her.

RACHEL   Three days ago I didn't know you. Now you've got your arms around me. And I can close my eyes and think how wonderful. How lovely this is, David. To have your arms around me. I think. I think I wanted them around me when I first met you. And in the restaurant, when you told me about wanting to be a writer, that's when I wanted to kiss you. And standing here, I feel your arms around me, your hands. I love the way you smell. I love the way you feel. I just don't want to open my eyes. 'Cause if I do, I'll look at your arm. Your hand. And that ring at the end of your finger. *(he takes his arms away)* I didn't mean for you to... *(as DAVID takes off his wedding ring)* Is it that easy?...David. Why are. This is crazy. Crazy.

DAVID   Rachel...

RACHEL	I looked in your wallet last night. I'm sorry. I shouldn't have. It's your wallet. It's your life. I don't have any business in either one.
DAVID	Don't be...
RACHEL	I couldn't sleep, I got up to write.
DAVID	Last night?
RACHEL	You were sound asleep. I know that, 'cause I. Must've been around four. Your pants were on the chair and I moved them and your wallet fell out. I. It's a nice shot, it's a nice picture of her. And the kids. How old are they?
DAVID	Uh. One's seven, the other's...Rachel...
RACHEL	You're so lucky. Let's go back.
DAVID	Rachel.
RACHEL	I need to do some...Okay?
DAVID	Okay. I'll um. I'll come in a minute.

She leaves. He puts the ring back on.

10. The lounge. JEFF and RACHEL.

JEFF	…So the Rabbi's wife says, "Be Gentile with me."…*(looking off)* Why would they put a pool downstairs from a bar?…How those rewrites comin?
RACHEL	Fantastic, it's…the whole thing's broken open, it's, it's…I think you *found* it, you identified what was *wrong* with it…
JEFF	No, no…
RACHEL	The—yes, please—the, the *language* and the, the way I was telling the story, I, it's got me thinking in ways I…
JEFF	Well. Alright, but that's you. I mean, I don't know how you do it. You sit there, you construct this *world* only to have people like me come and bust it up.
RACHEL	But I don't…
JEFF	And it's not just me. Are you kidding? Everybody knows how to write better than the writer. That's why, if you're gonna write a movie, if you're going to *create* something, you better have a good goddamned idea *why*. I mean, I'm not a writer, so. I'm curious. Do you do it because you *want* to, or because you *need* to?
RACHEL	I'm not sure I…see the difference.
JEFF	You would if you needed to. Why did you write "Zevi"?
RACHEL	Oh no. I tried to explain this to David.
JEFF	I'm not David.
RACHEL	Okay. Long time ago. The Jews, they get kicked out of Israel. They wander. They long to return. They develop the myth of the Messiah, a symbol of strength

	and hope. But that very symbol *prevents* them from acting, from returning to Israel.
JEFF	Like a Frank Capra film.
RACHEL	Yes it—what?
JEFF	Frank Capra...Jimmy Stewart: "Fuck you, Mr. Potter." Okay, he didn't say "fuck you," but but...Goes to Washington, whatever. Does the big speech to, to, the oppressor.
RACHEL	Uhh...
JEFF	The hero does the speech, does it up there on the big screen and we go, we, in the audience, go, "Hooray. Give it to him." Which absolves *us*...
RACHEL	Yes.
JEFF	Of, of...
RACHEL	Doing the speech, of...
JEFF	*Acting.*
RACHEL	Yes, yes. The Messiah acts on our behalf. It makes us weak because it says: one day, *he* will come for you. And when things get desperate enough, and some guy says: "I am *he*. Follow me," you don't question it. The followers of Zevi were desperate. And the followers of Zionism were desperate. After the Holocaust, they were vulnerable to *he* who said, "Let us return to Israel." They didn't question the return. They didn't question the morality of taking another people's land.
JEFF	I love it. I love that journey you just took me on.
RACHEL	Really?
JEFF	Really. The parallel with Israel, the whole thing. Fabulous.

RACHEL	You mean it?
JEFF	Fantastic. Except for one thing. It's not Zevi. It's Nathan.
RACHEL	Who, what, what do you mean?
JEFF	*He* was the guy. See. Zevi, he'd been doing the Messiah thing, only—nobody *cared.* They thought he was a *dick.* He wanted to give it up. So he goes to Gaza, 'cause he hears there's this young scholar, Nathan, who can heal souls.
RACHEL	Yes.
JEFF	Nathan looks at him, thinks, "This guy's got something I can use. I will convince him he is the Messiah." Nathan *sets him up.*
RACHEL	I'm…go on…
JEFF	Nathan didn't believe in miracles. He believed in work. Hard work. That's how you prepare for the coming of the Messiah. Right?
RACHEL	Yes. *Yes.*
JEFF	The only thing that went wrong for Nathan was the conversion. If Zevi had died, Nathan would have had a martyr. He would have started a whole new religion. Interesting, no?

DAVID enters with drinks.

JEFF	Whaja do, make it yourself?
DAVID	I got cornered by a hairdresser. She starts telling me about this screenplay about a bulemic stylist: Wash, Set and Hurl. I did the elk thing on her, she ran away. You believe what this place is turning into? A hairdressing convention.
JEFF	Bout time they got some real people in here.

DAVID	Everybody's got a story. Imagine that being yours. Here's your water.
RACHEL	Thanks.
DAVID	And your vodka.
RACHEL	No, no...
DAVID	Yes, yes.
RACHEL	It's a double.
DAVID	To "Zevi".
JEFF	To "Zevi".

They drink.

JEFF	*(to the room)* L'chaim, everybody! That's Jewish for: GET TO WORK. *(to DAVID and RACHEL)* Look at these fucking people. Artists. So proud of themselves. They're making *art.* Fuck does that mean?*(to an artist)* How ya doin, bud. *(to RACHEL and DAVID)* They come out here, they climb *mountains.*
DAVID	What's wrong with climbing mountains?
JEFF	They get *inspired.*
DAVID	You learn a lot climbing mountains.
JEFF	How about getting inspired by *people.* Look at 'em. They're cloistered. Cloistered. I'm walking around, listening in. "Oh, the cutbacks"..."Oh, the audience just doesn't understand"..."Oh the critics just don't"...Think they ever once say to themselves: "Hey. I'm not SPEAKING to anyone." They don't care. They hate the audience, hate 'em. Then they say, "Gimme money so I can make my art, which I don't give a shit if you understand." Here's a perfect example. *There* are the playwrights, *there* are the musicians, *there* are the...fuck are those? David, what are those?

DAVID   Wha—? Journalists.

JEFF   Journ—David.

DAVID   What?

JEFF   Look.

DAVID   Oh, fuck.

RACHEL   Wh…what?

DAVID   It's a…

JEFF   Fucking film critic from *The Globe*.

DAVID   Jeff…

JEFF   Let's kill him. C'mon. Throw him in the pool. Drown him. Who's gonna miss him? They'll promote the fucking baseball writer like they always do. What am I *doing* here? I gotta piss.

        JEFF leaves. DAVID and RACHEL sit there awhile. Finally:

RACHEL   I know what you mean about mountain climbing.

DAVID   Huh?

RACHEL   You think you see more clearly but in fact…well, you stand up there and you think you've figured something out but…

DAVID   But?

RACHEL   When I was in university, I met this guy. A sad looking man, really, but I found him attractive. He had a girlfriend. Well. Fiancee. She was studying out of town and…Well we ended up sleeping together. Me and him, I mean. We ended up doing a lot of things together. It was like he came to life, and so did I. He told me it was over between them. He told me their relationship was…stagnating. He told me they couldn't stand being with each other. He said, "When she comes home at Christmas, I'm gonna tell her about us." I'd been practically living with him by then. Sleeping in their bed. Her bed. I took over that place. He called me the day after Christmas. "I couldn't do it," he said. And he hung up. I said I'd never put myself in that position again. No, listen. David. What if…what am I gonna do if…if right now, I just say fuck it, it's over, it isn't "right," and in…ten years, twenty years I think, you idiot, why did you give it up?

> *JEFF comes back.*

JEFF	I'm curious: how does it work here. Like, do you do the work, David reads it, you go home?
RACHEL	Uhh…
JEFF	Or do you actually get to hear the words?
RACHEL	Well…
JEFF	'Cause I was thinking. I'm here, I'm interested. Why don't the three of us get together, sit in your room, read it.
DAVID	Whoa whoa…No. First of all: no. Second—You need more than three voices. I mean, there's scenes there with ten…
JEFF	So what?
DAVID	…twelve people speaking…
RACHEL	Not anymore.
DAVID	…it'd be too confusing… what?
RACHEL	I've. Taken out a lot of stuff. It's down to a hundred and thirty pages.
DAVID	You're kidding.

RACHEL	No. And, it's pretty much down to Zevi, Nathan and Sarah. And the Sultan.
DAVID	What about the followers?
RACHEL	I've sort of funneled them into Sarah, all their hopes and dreams into Sarah. I just found I...
DAVID	That's incredible, that's huge.
RACHEL	I mean they're not gone altogether. They're in the ghetto scenes and Constantinople and...
DAVID	Ghetto scenes?
JEFF	Here's what I think. It's Thursday. Take tomorrow, finish your work. Saturday, we'll sit in your room, read the damn thing.
RACHEL	David?
JEFF	I'll bring the lox if you bring the chains.
DAVID	Could I at least see it first?
RACHEL	Sure. Uhh...Well. Guess I have some work to do.
DAVID	Lemme walk you back.
JEFF	She's a big girl, she can walk herself back.
DAVID	W—I just. I thought um. I might look at some of what you've done now.
JEFF	David: we need to talk. You've been avoiding me for two days.
RACHEL	Well, if you want to come by after...
DAVID	Yeah...that's...I'll swing by and look at what you've done.
RACHEL	Yeah. I'll uh... leave the door open. Night, Jeff.

JEFF   Sh'long.

                    Exit RACHEL.

JEFF   Okay. Rewrites.

DAVID   Rewrites?

JEFF   Earl's rewrites. Now hold on. Before you say one word. Can I just say to you what I went through to get you these rewrites.

DAVID   Jeff, I...

JEFF   The second you're outta the office, I'm on the phone with Earl, readin him the fucking riot act. I said— hello?

DAVID   I'm listening.

JEFF   I'm tellin a story. I said, "David wants this and David wants that." Know what he says? "What are you, David's mess-en-ger?" That's right. "Well, tell your Boss" — this is Earl — "tell your *boss* he wouldn't know a good screenplay if it crawled up his ass."

DAVID   What?

JEFF   "If it crawled..."

DAVID   That prick.

JEFF   Listen. I said, "You think you're special? You're nothing. We got a contract gives us the option to go with another writer. David is doing you a favour keeping you around this long. You're lucky we didn't farm it out six drafts ago. Now you give us the goddamn changes we agreed to a year-and-a-half ago or we're gonna *take* the goddamn option."

DAVID   "If it crawled up his ass."

JEFF   Wouldya forget about that? He goes, "Talk to my
             agent." So I do. Ten minutes later schmuck-boy calls
             me. "Tell me what you need." I go to his house, stick
             the play down next the computer. "I wanna see every
             word of this play on that computer screen. Only I want
             you to make these characters more human. This is
             what David wants, and what David wants, David is
             gonna get." Know what he did?

DAVID   What?

JEFF   Started to cry. Like this. "I can't do it. I don't have it
             in me." I go, "Sure you do, Earl. Come on. Start
             digging. Humanize 'em, you fuck." So he dug. I'm
             tellin ya, I'm like a page turner for like at a piano
             recital. I sat there and watched him write every line.
             It's all there: the scene with the shrink, the whole bit,
             not one false step. And this. This is what I gave you,
             made *to order*. Alright? So?

DAVID   It ain't there.

JEFF   "Ain't there"?

DAVID   I told you. I'm not interested. Go home.

JEFF   And let you ruin the company for a fuck manuscript?

DAVID   It's not a fuck manuscript. I read it before I met her.

JEFF   What's the difference?

DAVID   I'm leaving Jen.

JEFF   ...You're what?

DAVID   I'm leaving Jennifer. When I get back home, I'm
             leaving her. Rachel and I are gonna be together. And
             we are gonna make her movie.

JEFF   She's a fucking *wannabe*.

DAVID   She's not a wannabe. She's for real.

JEFF	Open your fucking eyes.
DAVID	Lower your voice.
JEFF	Why, so the rest of these fucking wannabes won't hear me? I give two shits about these fuckers? Listen. You got people counting on you. Waiting for you. For your decision.
DAVID	I've made it.
JEFF	We spent fifteen years waiting for this chance.
DAVID	You don't understand.
JEFF	You're fucking right I don't.
DAVID	I have to be with her. I *have* to...
JEFF	Do you understand what you're doing?
DAVID	No.
JEFF	No. David. *David.* What can I do? How can I help you?
DAVID	You can go home.

DAVID gets up.

JEFF	Go back to your room, David. Two more days and you never have to see this woman again. And in a week, a month, you'll see, you'll remember, you'll think, What was I doing? I almost gave it up, for *her?* Go back to your room.

DAVID leaves.

11. RACHEL's room. The next morning. DAVID is staring at her.

RACHEL   *(waking up)* What are you lookin at?…What are you dressed for?

DAVID   I gotta meet Phil.

RACHEL   Mm.

DAVID   You wanna take a break later? I thought we'd drive out to the lake.

RACHEL   Sure.

DAVID   You have to see this lake. It's green. And still. There's another spot I like, about a half hour drive. You walk for a while, then there's this cave, and on the other side, a waterfall. It's fabulous, the spray hits your face, you can—Shit. I can't.

RACHEL   Why?

DAVID   There's a faculty dinner tonight. How about tomorrow?

RACHEL   Do you have to meet Phil?

DAVID   We both have to work. Is it half past? I gotta call Jen. You gonna show me these new pages tonight?

RACHEL   Uh huh. David?

DAVID   Yeah?

RACHEL   When we get back to the city…

DAVID   Yeah…

RACHEL   I mean. Go meet Phil.

DAVID   No. Say it.

RACHEL	What's gonna happen? How does this…whatever this is…how does it…
DAVID	Rachel. Listen to me. I'm leaving Jennifer.
RACHEL	David, I…
DAVID	Listen. What did yesterday tell you? You said this was crazy. Well we're here now. We have to be together. I got it all figured out. We'll get an apartment. A house. With a couple of extra rooms for the kids.
RACHEL	What kids?
DAVID	My kids. A place by the lake. You like the Beach? I love it down there. Cept on the weekends. Anyway. We'll go for walks on the boardwalk. With a big, you know, one of those, those dogs everybody's got down there.
RACHEL	One of those dogs.
DAVID	They're brown and…whatever. You know what I mean. You'll have a studio. In the loft.
RACHEL	Uh huh.
DAVID	We're gonna be a team. I'm gonna produce your scripts. "Zevi"'s just the first. It's gonna do the Festival circuit, get your name out there. They're gonna love this in Cannes, I'm tellin ya. Sundance, Vienna, Berlin. Rachel.
RACHEL	You are a salesman.
DAVID	Is it just me?
RACHEL	No. I want to be with you.
DAVID	Then. When we get back. I'm just gonna need a little time to…
RACHEL	David…

DAVID   Listen, to sort things out with Jen...

RACHEL   I can't...

DAVID   Listen. This is my decision. Alright? Rachel. We know what this is. Why should we give it up? Things happen. This happened. That's it. Kiss me.

RACHEL   This is so...

DAVID   Kiss me.

                      She brings him into bed. His cell phone rings.

DAVID   I don't think I'll answer that. But I have to go. I'll see you in a few hours, alright? I'll see ya.

                      He exits.

RACHEL   See ya. See ya. See ya.

12. RACHEL's room. That afternoon.

RACHEL   *(on the phone)* Dad, let me finish…*(reading from paper)* "The United States said arrangements were being made for a large White House ceremony on Monday, when Israel and the PLO will sign a companion agreement to introduce Palestinian self-rule to Israeli-occupied territories"…

      Enter JEFF.

      Dad…I'll call you tonight…alright…before bed…alright, then…goodbye. *(she hangs up)*

JEFF   You leave your door unlocked.

RACHEL   Sometimes. How are you?

JEFF   Good. How's the writing?

RACHEL   Pretty good, I think.

JEFF   Those changes coming along?

RACHEL   They're fantastic. You wanna see what I did with…

JEFF   I'll wait. You seen David?

RACHEL   David? No. Why?

JEFF   Why what?

RACHEL   Why would I have seen David?

JEFF   He said he was gonna drop by last night.

RACHEL   Oh. Right.

JEFF   To look at the rewrites.

RACHEL   Yes.

JEFF	Did he?
RACHEL	No. Yes.
JEFF	Uh huh. Rachel. I know what's going on here.
RACHEL	What's going on. Here?
JEFF	I have to say this. I want to say this for your own protection. Okay? Because he loves his wife. It's a fact. He's never going to leave her.
RACHEL	I don't see what…
JEFF	I can *see* what's happening here. Look. David wants…it's obvious what David wants, and what David wants, David gets. Always.
RACHEL	Not always.
JEFF	Well, if that's true, that's good.
RACHEL	I don't really think…
JEFF	It's any of my business. But it is. David wants one thing: to fuck you, alright? I'm sorry to be so…that's *it*. You think he wants to make your film? I'm *sorry*.
RACHEL	Look, Jeff…
JEFF	I'm saying this to help you.
RACHEL	I think I can handle—
JEFF	You're wrong. Because I've seen what he does. Look. He's in a very powerful position. He likes that. He uses that. He's done it to other writers. Never mind the actresses.
RACHEL	What are you tell—
JEFF	It's a *problem*. I happen to have some knowledge of this. I happen to…forget it.

RACHEL   Well, you've started, you might as well finish.

JEFF   Lake Charlotte.

RACHEL   That movie?

JEFF   It isn't a movie. It happened. David's wife, Leah? We were engaged.

RACHEL   You and...?

JEFF   That's right. The three of us went away together, to plan the business. Leah went there as *my* fiancee, left as David's. They've been together ever since, like this. Nothing's gonna break them up. She has affairs, he has affairs, they're the fucking misery twins, they love it, it fuels them, they fuck somebody else, feel like shit for doing it, make a big confession, have a big fight, fuck like dogs for months, start the whole cycle all over again.

RACHEL   Why did—? I mean, why are you still partners?

JEFF   What was I gonna do? They *love* each other. It wasn't for me to do anything about it. I felt like shit for a while, got over it, big deal, you go on. Listen, Rachel. I think you're fantastic, I really do, I think you're clever and funny and attractive and. I don't want to see happen to you what's happened to. A lot of girls. Women. One night, some awards show, he was pissed. "Jeff," he said this, he said, "Jeff, you've got one great love in your life. You have to learn how to recognise her." He was looking right at Leah, standing across the room. Buncha guys around her. She's a beautiful woman. He can't stand being away from her. He's probably on the phone with her right now....

RACHEL   Why. Are you telling me.

JEFF   Don't believe him. Whatever he tells you. Alright?

RACHEL   I really think. You've got the wrong. Idea.

JEFF   Did he tell you he was gonna leave his wife?

RACHEL   You really don't know what you're talking about.

JEFF   "It's over." Did he say that?

RACHEL   David and I have a very. Professional.

JEFF   "What colour are your eyes," did he say that?

RACHEL   He's my teacher and.

JEFF   "Step into the light."

RACHEL   I'm here, for a week, as a writer.

JEFF   "Let me look at your eyes."

RACHEL   To. To....Stupid. Stupid. *Stupid.*

JEFF   *(going to her)* It's al—I'm sorry. Look. It'd be a lot
worse if it went any further, you know?

　　　　　He leaves; she starts working.

13. *RACHEL at her desk. DAVID at RACHEL's*
door. He knocks.

DAVID   Rachel?...Rrrrrrachel?...Sho, open up....Vat, are you
shleeping? I brought a little nosh from the fekulty
party. Rachela?

He knocks again then scrapes the door with his
fingers.

Raaaaaaachellllll...open uuuuuuuup...

Open the pod bay door, Hal.

Alright, my pretty. But I'll get those ruby slippers.
Yeah, and your little dog, too.

He walks away. She types.

14. *Next day. RACHEL's room. DAVID, JEFF,
and RACHEL are reading from the screenplay of
"Zevi".*

JEFF   *"Why have you forsaken us?" A Cossack slashes his
throat. Cut to: Exterior. Day. Top of a mountain.
Zevi, Nathan and Sarah at their mountain retreat.*

David.

DAVID   Mm.

JEFF   You reading?

DAVID   What, yeah.

JEFF   You're reading Zevi, right.

DAVID   Yeah. Uhh...*their mountain retreat...* "*Everywhere, the
children of Israel are hunted...unwanted, unloved,
powerless, helpless...they look to me for guidance but
I do not know where to lead them. They say, 'Waken
the dead, Messiah, bring back my father who the
Cossacks murdered, my sister whose body the
Cossacks desecrated.' Nathan, I can't perform miracles.
I'm a man. I'm only a man. A weakling, a liar.*"

JEFF   *"Messiah, the people do not need miracles. They only
need your words. They will perform the miracles
themselves, but only if they believe in themselves.
That is your purpose, Messiah. That is your tikkun."*

DAVID   *"I am afraid."*

JEFF   *"Rabbi, we are all afraid. Lead us into Israel, and we
will no longer be afraid. We will have our own
kingdom at last, at last, at long last. It is you,
Messiah. You are he. You are he who will lead us into
Israel."*

DAVID   *"What of the Arabs who now live there?"*

JEFF	*"They will be sent out from the land, for the land is ours, the land was given us by God when he retreated from the world and left his light in the sky. Messiah. The people are waiting. Do not abandon them. Do not abandon Torah. Torah is your love. Your one true love." Close up on Zevi. His eyes change to those of a man entering a trance; Zevi is in a state of illumination. The doubt is gone. He sees a vision of the future.*
DAVID	*"Yes, Nathan. Now is the time."*
JEFF	*Cut to Sarah's tent. Enter Nathan. "It is done. He will go to Constantinople. He will be martyred. And you and I will be together, Sarah."*
DAVID	What?
RACHEL	Something wrong?
DAVID	Wh—wh—where is this going?
JEFF	Come on, David. Give it a chance.
DAVID	Do you mind?...I'm sorry. Sorry. Let's uhh. Go on.
JEFF	*Cut to Zevi's tent. On his bed, a Torah scroll.*
	David?
DAVID	Uhhh..."Oh my love. I have left Sarah for you, my love. For you are my one true love. The time has come. To consummate our. Love?"
JEFF	Come on, David. You can read better than that. *Cut back to Sarah and Nathan. "Soon the spark of every Jewish soul will ascend to heaven. Israel will be ours. We must commit tikkun, Sarah. You and I. Our souls need to be mended. Together. Come, Sarah, mend my soul." They move toward each other.*
RACHEL	*"Nathan."*

JEFF	*"Sarah." They kiss. Cut back to Zevi. He is naked. He caresses the Torah, removes its covering, as though undressing it.*
RACHEL	David, do you mind?
DAVID	What?
RACHEL	You're *sighing*.
JEFF	*He spreads the scrolls, caresses the parchment.*
	Alright, who's reading Torah?
DAVID	The Torah speaks?
JEFF	HE'S A MYSTIC.
RACHEL	I'll read it.
RACHEL	*"Do you love me, Zevi?"*
DAVID	*"I love your words. Your Holy Words. Let me touch your words. Let me kiss them."*
RACHEL	*"You love my words. But do you love me?"*
DAVID	*"I do."*
RACHEL	*"And you will never abandon me?"*
DAVID	*"Never."*
RACHEL	*"Then hold me, Zevi. Hold me and never let me go."*
JEFF	*Cut to Sarah and Nathan, naked, on the bed.*
RACHEL	*"Hold me, Nathan. Hold me and never let me go. It is you I love, not Zevi. It is you."*
JEFF	*"And I you." Cut to Zevi, wrapped in the Torah.*
DAVID	*"I am God. I am God. I am…"*

RACHEL   There's more…

DAVID   I think that's enough for now. Okay. Umm…Jeff, would you excuse us?

RACHEL   I want Jeff to stay.

DAVID   We need to talk.

RACHEL   Talk.

DAVID   About the script. Jeff, do you mind?

RACHEL   I said I want him to stay.

DAVID   Alright. Well. I have to say it's. It's not what I expected um. I uhh. Was a little surprised to see all the references to Israel. I thought we'd decided to…

RACHEL   We didn't decide anything. That's not the way you work, remember?

DAVID   Yeah. Okay. We can get to that. Um. The ghetto scenes. I find them. Disturbing. The ripping open of the woman's belly…and the cat, I…Where did that come from?

RACHEL   It happened.

DAVID   I know, but it was more effective when it was only alluded to.

RACHEL   It needed to be more visceral.

DAVID   *(looking at JEFF)* "More visceral." I see. Um. Which, which would you say is the A plot?

RACHEL   The love story.

DAVID   Uh huh.

RACHEL   Look, if you don't like it, just tell me.

DAVID   I…

RACHEL   You're attacking everything, everything.

DAVID   I think you're…

RACHEL   If you think it's a piece of shit, just say so. Don't pat
              me on the back. Don't *nurture* me, that's such crap, I
              want to know what you think, love it, hate it, I don't
              care, just tell me the truth for once for fuck's sake.

DAVID   …Would you excuse me for a second?

                        He leaves. Silence. After a moment he returns.

DAVID   Okay. I'm not gonna say anything. You tell me.
              Because obviously I don't get it. What were you trying
              to do with the revisions?

RACHEL   I was trying to make it more human.

DAVID   Oh. So…Zevi loves Torah, Nathan loves Sarah, Sarah
              loves Nathan—Jerusalem 90210, that's, that's more
              human? *Well.* I'm asking you…is that…?

RACHEL   I don't know.

DAVID   You think we're fooling around here?

JEFF   Woops.

DAVID   Shut the fuck up.

RACHEL   Is this your way of "being here for me"?

DAVID   I *am* here for you. I just, I don't understand these
              changes, these, and the poetry, what happened to
              the…"what of the Arabs who," what is that?

RACHEL   I was trying something different. If you didn't want to
              see something different, you…This is bullshit.
              Bullshit.

                        She leaves.

JEFF   *(looking out the window)* There goes that elk again.

DAVID   I oughta stuff this down your throat, one page at a
            time.

JEFF   Kiss me first.

DAVID   You asshole.

JEFF   *Hey.* She asked *me.* Alright? There you go: your "real
            writers," your "real people." You like what she did?
            Huh? You think she's a writer? She's a wannabe, she
            can't do the work, she's got no craft.

DAVID   I didn't get a chance to help her.

JEFF   Definition of a wannabe: a writer who gives you
            exactly what you ask for. I gave her some notes.
            What'd she do? Put 'em down word for word. Now quit
            fuckin the Torah and let's go home.

DAVID   You're poison, you know that?

JEFF   Everybody's a critic.

DAVID   She has to go back to what she had.

JEFF   Good advice, take it yourself.

DAVID   Fuck's that supposed to mean?

JEFF   Means this. You want to fuck up your marriage, I can't
            stop you. You want to fuck up the company, I can't let
            you. You want to make this piece of shit Jew art pic,
            go ahead. You wanna live the rest of your life making
            films gonna play the Carlton for a week, go ahead. You
            want to let down about fifty people waiting on this
            thing, go ahead. You want to live with the rumours and
            the gossip, go ahead. The company is going with Earl's
            script. It's happening. We are commited.

DAVID   What are you...

JEFF   You want to come with me, tell me right now.

DAVID   What are you talking...

JEFF	You don't, good fucking luck to you.
DAVID	What are you talking about?
JEFF	I'm talking about sixty-forty. As in your forty. My sixty.*(shows him a fax)*
DAVID	*(looks it over)* When did this happen?
JEFF	While you were sleeping. Around.
DAVID	Jesus. *(makes call on cell phone)*
JEFF	You are in deep shit. I could walk out on you right now.
DAVID	Shut up.
JEFF	I could leave you in the shit right now.
DAVID	I said shut up.
JEFF	But I'm gonna give you one more chance. Earl or Zevi. Right now. You choose.
DAVID	I said shut the fuck up! What are you doing to me? I'm staying here! Right—*(into phone)* Jen?…Okay…. What is going on?…uh huh…yes…it's not about…she's 33…it's not about that…it's not about "is she more beautiful," it's…I can't talk about this right now…we're talking about the business, just stick to the…Jen…

Enter RACHEL.

…you can rip it up….yes you can…it's not legal yet…I can't say that…I can't say that right now…Jenny…Jen I…no…don't, don't put…hi, sweetheart…how are ya?…uh huh…yes, I'm in the mountains…oh, lots of bears, lots and…I miss you too, sweetheart…soon…very soon…put mummy back…okay…well you…I'll see you soon….Bye bye…

He hangs up.

DAVID	…Um…I um…need to…talk…
JEFF	David. I'm going.
RACHEL	*(to DAVID)* I think you should go.
DAVID	*(to JEFF)* I need to talk…
RACHEL	I think it's be best if…
DAVID	*(to RACHEL)* Can I talk to you?
RACHEL	If…
JEFF	I'm going.
DAVID	*(to JEFF)* I *need* to TALK TO YOU.
RACHEL	I want you to leave.
DAVID	I'm not LEAVING.
JEFF	I'm gone.

Exit JEFF; RACHEL starts packing.

DAVID	What…what are you doing?
RACHEL	What's it look like?
DAVID	Where you going?
RACHEL	Home, David.
DAVID	Home? *Home?* Look, I'm sorry, about what I said.
RACHEL	No, you're right. The changes are awful.
DAVID	Can we forget about the script for a…
RACHEL	What else have we got?

DAVID	Why do you, why do you say that? What's… You didn't look at me the whole time. I was at your door half a dozen times last night, you didn't…Are you backing off?…Oh this is…this is funny? I'm dying here.
RACHEL	*You're* dying.
DAVID	I just want to hold you. I want to lie down with you. I want to be with you, every second, I can't think, I can't stop thinking, about you, and.
RACHEL	I thought, too…
DAVID	I don't like the sound of that.
RACHEL	Why did you tell me, remember, yesterday morning, you had to call your wife?
DAVID	I said that?
RACHEL	I thought it was funny you'd say that.
DAVID	Is that what this is?…Rachel. I was figuring out my day. Rachel…
RACHEL	It's over, David.
DAVID	…No…
RACHEL	Go back to your life.
DAVID	No.
RACHEL	Your wife.
DAVID	*No.* My marriage is over. I'm leaving Jennifer, *leaving* her. At the faculty party last night, I just, I wanted you to be there, to see you, across the room, to watch you…
RACHEL	What did she want you to say?
DAVID	Who?

RACHEL	Your WIFE. "I can't say that right now,' what, what was that?
DAVID	This isn't about her. This is about *this,* here, I...I need you...I *need...*
RACHEL	Oh, you're full of shit. I've heard it. You've said it before, you've said it before and never meant it. It's just words, lies...
DAVID	What are you talking...?
RACHEL	I know you. I was *told.* You *do* this. This is *something* you *do,* all the *time.*
DAVID	This?
RACHEL	Fall in love. For a week. A couple of days. Then it's back to your wife.
DAVID	I do *not* do this all the time. What I have done is fallen for a woman, been *nuts* about a woman and done *nothing,* and this time, this time I'm going to do something about it, I am not going to let it...*please,* Rachel. I'm going to leave her.
RACHEL	"Her"? You mean Jeff's fiancee. Who became your wife.
DAVID	Okay. That's what this is. What happened is this: Jen had feelings for me, before she and Jeff got engaged. The three of us went to Lake Charlotte, she told me how she felt about me.
RACHEL	You had nothing to do with it.
DAVID	I told you. She had these feelings.
RACHEL	And you had none.
DAVID	I put them away. What was I gonna do with them? When she confided in me, then, *yes,* of course, I, I had the same feelings.
RACHEL	Which are now gone.

DAVID	They were never that strong.
RACHEL	Oh, Jesus.
DAVID	I know what I feel for you. And with Jen, it's gone. There's nothing there. No passion, no—
RACHEL	Don't say passion when you're talking about love.
DAVID	I'm in *love* with you.
RACHEL	You're in love with your wife and maybe, maybe right *now* there's no passion but.
DAVID	None.
RACHEL	You can't sustain passion for years, you'd be *dead.*
DAVID	I am. Dead, I am dead. I was. But now, Rachel, you've, it's like all this passion I have, inside me, my capacity for loving someone...
RACHEL	Don't...
DAVID	My capacity for it, I'm saying, and the emotions of, and the physical, the changes going on inside me, coming out of me, it's amazing, these feelings, someone taking over, devouring you, not letting you sleep or eat...I understand now, what my life is, empty, without those feelings, I've been walking around dead, and now, you've brought me back from the dead...
RACHEL	Don't turn me into something...
DAVID	I need you, Rachel...
RACHEL	Don't turn me into something I can't, won't be. I believed it, David. I believed it when you told me you wanted out of your old life. And I thought, yes, *yes,* I'm the *one* who...and there was...there *was...what the fuck is it...*do you have any idea, David...Do you know what it's like to be set up like that, to be told you're the *one* and to be left alone?

DAVID	Of course I do.
RACHEL	After the promise of eternal love.
DAVID	You think I haven't been left behind?
RACHEL	It's different for men.
DAVID	What?
RACHEL	It's different. You find someone else, someone younger, always someone else, and it won't matter to you, because you're always looking, always leaving, always running away. You'll leave me alone and what'll I have? Nothing. And I'll try to to fall asleep and wake up each morning with this one inconsolable fact: I have been left behind. I wasn't good enough. I wasn't good enough for *him.* I wasn't beautiful enough, wasn't dutiful enough. That's it, isn't it? That's the magic formula. Yes, you want me at your side at *screenings* at at *faculty parties*, you want me to stand on the other side of the room while men ogle so you can feel powerful. Then your eyes'll shift and you'll see someone else, someone else who'll make you feel *alive,* David. Is that what you need? Someone to make you feel alive? Well there'll always be someone, David. Someone to make you feel alive for a day, a week, a month, 'til you get bored and then what? Someone else, always someone else. I don't want that. And I don't want to be the one who lets you do that to someone else. You go back to your wife. I know men like you. You need a great love. You have it, she's sitting there by the phone and your children are asleep and they need...you prick...you've got something the rest of us spend our whole lives wishing for, and you're willing to give it up for what, for nothing.
DAVID	You think this is nothing? I just. I just gave everything up for you. To be with you. To...
RACHEL	No you didn't. You gave it up for you. It's all about you. This whole thing is about *you.* Well.*(gives him a paper)* Here. I wrote this for you.

DAVID   What?

RACHEL   I wrote it last night. With you in mind.

DAVID   What is it?

RACHEL   It's another scene.

DAVID   I don't want to read the—

RACHEL   *Interior. Night. Sultan's chambers. Zevi is in Muslim garb. He holds the Torah....*Read it.

DAVID   *"Torah, my love, there is one great love. Only one. In one's lifetime. And we must find it. Or we will be lost, all our lives. Though we shared a bed, you are not my great love. My great love is myself. I love no one, Torah. No one, but myself."*

    Why?

RACHEL   Because everyone acts from self-interest...because people throw around words like love without...because people...because men...no...because people...Because people are afraid...they act out of fear...of being alone...and they don't realise...that every act is a betrayal of someone else...that every betrayal puts out one more spark...creates one more lost soul...takes us further away from tikkun...the mending...peace...the Messiah will never come...because people are selfish...because people...deserve each other, and our misery, for ever and ever. Get out..

DAVID   Get out? You've fucked everything up. Shit, we got work to do. Lots of work to do. Alright. Story meeting.

RACHEL   Don't do this.

DAVID   It's awkwardly written, stylistically inconsistent, just one embarrassingly bad scene after another. There are so many flaws in it I don't see how you can save it. Why am I wasting my time? Whatever gave you the idea you were a writer, an *artist?* You think anyone's gonna be interested in some melodrama about a bunch of fucked-up Jews? Listen. Why don't you do us all a favour and go back to teaching Hebrew school, or whatever it is you think you can do best, because it's obvious to me that the one thing you can't do, shouldn't do, is write, and, listen—Rachel, is it?— *Rachela:* I'd like to leave the retreat knowing I've done a service, so, let me hear you say something, 'cause I don't want to lead you astray; I don't want to give you any false hope; I want to hear you say: "I'm not a writer." Do me a favour, "I'm not a writer," say it, *"I am not a writer." SAY IT.*

15. The lounge.

JEFF   *(on cell phone)* Earl, don't worry about it...he's not gonna do the bus movie...because he's doing *Hamlet* in January...yeah...in Winnipeg...I know...now the thing is, I just talked to his people in L.A....Erwin Stoff, 3 Arts...He's got a couple of concerns we're still waiting to hear from Winona's people, but lemme run something else by you: whaddaya think of Jennifer Jason Leigh for the courier?...who?...who?...What, from that lawyer show?...gimme a break, we need stars, pal...the Americans'd never go for it...we need 'B' list or higher friend...we're in the big leagues, boy...well, thank you, Earl, I'll take it under advisement.

Enter DAVID.

...Gotta go.

JEFF hangs up and waits for DAVID.

DAVID   Jeff. I made a mistake. Please. Let me come back. Let me come back.

JEFF   Beg me.

DAVID   I am begging you.

JEFF   On your knees.

DAVID   What?

JEFF   David. I ruined three marriages for this company. I lost every friend I ever had for this company. I lied to people, I cheated people, I screwed them. I built this company from nothing. And every day I watched you getting credit for it. Every party I went to, it was, "How's David doing? My God, he works hard." Come on, David. Beg me. *(DAVID stays standing)*   Fuck you.

JEFF leaves.

16. *A classroom in Toronto.*

RACHEL   Good morning children. Shana Tova.

I have something to read to you.

"I am truly sorry for the words I spoke last semester, when I equated Jewish settlers living in Judea and Samaria with terrorists. Clearly, this was wrong. If I have misled any of you, forgive me. If I have caused any of you to suffer in any way for my ill-spoken words, forgive me."

Well. I think that's enough about Israel.

This year we are going to study Jewish mysticism.

Take out your notebooks.

17. *JEFF's office.*

JEFF   *(on phone)* …proves what a schmuck-and-a-half he is, ends up living alone with nothing.…What happens to Nathan?…He uhh, does okay…whaddaya think, Earl, you think you can do this?…Oh, squeeze me, it's "not your thing."…Eh?…What?…Oh, yeah, what rumour's that?…Where'd'ya hear that?…No it isn't…No he did not have "a nervous breakdown."…Oh, pardon me, Earl, I guess you know more about David Fine than I do…Now you wanna know the truth or you wanna go around slinging this bullshit? 'Cause the truth is he left the business because he couldn't stand making pieces of crap scripts like *yours*. Okay? That is the truth. So next time I call you up and offer you something might represent a bit of a CHALLENGE, maybe you oughta think about what YOUR THING is and what YOUR THING might be, and not be so quick to make judgments on people who know a fuck of a lot more about this world than you do. You got it?…Good. 'Cause I hear one more word from you about David Fine, I'm gonna…So long, Earl.

He hangs up.

18. Toronto. The Bialik Centre.

WOLF	Who's there?
DAVID	Mr. Benjamin?
WOLF	Who is it? I don't see so good.
DAVID	Mr. Benjamin, my name is David Fine.
WOLF	Fine. Did you say Fine?
DAVID	Yes, sir. I'm a friend of—
WOLF	You know Yetta?
DAVID	Yetta...
WOLF	Are you the Fines from Montreal?
DAVID	No. We're—I'm not.
WOLF	Then what are you talking, you wouldn't know Yetta. She died.
DAVID	I'm sorry.
WOLF	What are you sorry? This is fifty years ago. So? Who are you?
DAVID	I'm a friend of your daughter.
WOLF	Which one? I got a big mishpucha.
DAVID	Have you.
WOLF	You know what that is?
DAVID	Family.
WOLF	Good boy.

DAVID	I'm a friend of Rachel.
WOLF	You know my Rachela?
DAVID	A little. We spent some time together.
WOLF	Oh?
DAVID	Coupla months ago. At a writer's retreat, she...
WOLF	Oh. David Fine.
DAVID	Yes.
WOLF	Sure. I know you. My daughter told me all about you. Come a little closer.
DAVID	Has Rachel been in today?
WOLF	She usually gets here five. You can wait in here if you want.
DAVID	How's she doing?
WOLF	Okay.
DAVID	She back at school?
WOLF	Well. She's not a writer is she?
DAVID	How are you feeling?
WOLF	Terrific.
DAVID	Rachel told me about the...
WOLF	Tumour? It's just a word, Mr Fine. You won't get one if you say it.
DAVID	Rachel told me some stories. About your life, in Israel.
WOLF	Yeah?

DAVID	About how much you love Israel. How you'd like to go back.
WOLF	I don't want to go back.
DAVID	Oh.
WOLF	That isn't my country anymore.
DAVID	Well...
WOLF	You see what they're doing? Handing over the land.
DAVID	Yes, I...
WOLF	They're retreating. You can't retreat. Not for a second. You do and you're dead. Because you've given up. That's it. Soon, there won't be an Israel no more, and we'll go into exile again.
DAVID	Can I ask you something?
WOLF	You got a mouth.
DAVID	Why did you leave? Israel.
WOLF	I had my reasons.
DAVID	Can you tell me?
WOLF	Why would I tell you?
DAVID	Well. I'm. I want to tell your story. I'm writing a movie.
WOLF	Are you? About my life?
DAVID	Can I tell you? It's about the search for peace. It's about a man who gives his life for his country. And his country betrays him. Does this interest you?
WOLF	Go on, Mr. Fine.

DAVID	He leaves his country. Turns his back on it. He loves this country, never wants to leave it, but he's compelled to. He goes to another country. Only he never feels at home there. As he grows older, he comes to realise that his home, his true home, is all he has, that he wants to return to it. He wants to see this country once more before he dies. The thing is, he doesn't know anymore which is his true home. He can't be sure....What time does Rachel usually come by?
WOLF	Any time. Go on with your story.
DAVID	He wonders, did he ever have a home? Will he ever have a home? As he recalls his life, we see it, in flashbacks. The creation of Israel. Coming to Canada.
WOLF	Through *my* life.
DAVID	That's right. The thing is. I need to know. Why you...No. Not why you...What I need to know is: have you ever regretted not going back?
WOLF	Never.
DAVID	Right. Well. That's good.
WOLF	Now I got a question for you.
DAVID	Alright.
WOLF	Do you believe me?
DAVID	I. Did Rachel tell you what happened? Between us, I mean?
WOLF	A little.
DAVID	Well. Tell her I said hello, would you?
WOLF	Tell her yourself.
DAVID	I can't. I'm sorry.

WOLF	You're lost, Mr. Fine.
DAVID	You have no idea.
WOLF	You'll find your way.
DAVID	Thanks. *(he starts to go)*
WOLF	I met a woman.
DAVID	What?
WOLF	A Canadian girl. I fell in love with her. She was there for the summer. Working on a kibbutz. We met at a dance. Oh, she was beautiful. The most beautiful woman. The whole summer we spent together; you couldn't get us apart. Then she had to go home. I had to choose. I chose to go with her. Rachel's mother. She was thirty-five when she died. Thirty-five, Mr. Fine. There's not a day I don't think about her. There's not a day I don't remember the first time I saw her. I can't go back. I'm afraid I'll see her everywhere I go. You want to know did I ever regret? What can I tell you, Mr. Fine? I can sit here and regret never coming; or I could be sitting in Israel regretting never having left. You still want to tell my story?
DAVID	If I come here, everyday, with a tape recorder...
WOLF	You like herring?
DAVID	Not especially.
WOLF	I do.
DAVID	It's yours.
WOLF	When do we start?
DAVID	Monday?
WOLF	The sooner the better, don't you think?
DAVID	Right. Well. Tell Rachel I dropped by.

WOLF   Tell her yourself.

DAVID   *(turns; sees RACHEL)* Hello Rachel.

RACHEL   What are you doing here?

DAVID   I...

RACHEL   You've got no right to be here.

WOLF   He was talking to me.

RACHEL   Dad.

WOLF   He's gonna make my life a movie. I'm gonna talk into
              a machine, tell him the whole megilluh.

RACHEL   You're gonna *what?*

WOLF   Tell him my life.

RACHEL   That's what you're doing here?

DAVID   No. I just...

RACHEL   You just what?

DAVID   Wanted to...

RACHEL   Look, David...

DAVID   I just...

RACHEL   There's really nothing...

DAVID   Just...

RACHEL   There's *nothing*...

DAVID   Rachel, please. *Please.*

              *DAVID walks away; WOLF gestures RACHEL
              to join DAVID.*

DAVID   I left my wife.

RACHEL   Is that what you came to tell me?

DAVID   No. I...

RACHEL   I know. "I've been thinking about you, I hope you're doing alright."

DAVID   Will you give me a chance?

RACHEL   How many you think you got?

DAVID   I came to apologise.

RACHEL   Yeah? Well?

DAVID   I'm sorry.

RACHEL   Great. Do I throw my arms around you *now?*

DAVID   I'm trying.

RACHEL   What are you trying?

DAVID   Trying. Trying to live my life the way I. Yes, I was thinking about you. Yes, I was thinking about the first time I saw you. About, about standing on the mountain with my arms around you, about how everything inside me changed. I can't forget that. I don't want to forget that. And I don't want you to think I was lying when...Look. I didn't come here thinking we'd somehow get together. I don't even know if that's possible, for either one of us, I. I just want to do good.

RACHEL   So you come here, you use my father as a pretext to see me, and that's good?

DAVID   It's not a pretext, I...

RACHEL   You think I can believe a word you say, David? You don't want to for*get*. Well I do. So if you want to do good, stay away from me. That would be "good." In fact. It would be great. Okay?

DAVID starts to go.

WOLF   Mr. Fine. I'll see you Monday?

DAVID   I'll be here.

WOLF   Don't forget the. Tape recorder.

DAVID   I won't forget.

DAVID leaves.

WOLF   Rachel, you there?

RACHEL   Yeah.

WOLF   Come. Come here. Sit. You think you're alone.

RACHEL   I don't just think it.

WOLF   You're not alone, Rachela. You got your family. Your friends. Your children. A whole city, filled with things to do. You'll go out, be with people.

RACHEL   I've had enough of people.

WOLF   This man, David Fine. Thinks I'm doing him a favour, telling him my stories? He doesn't know. It's for you. A little present.

RACHEL   A present.

WOLF   Rachela. What can you do? You spend your whole life looking for something; one day, there it is. And you're happy. Next day, gone. Alright. So what are you gonna do? Stop living? Or be thankful you had it, even for a moment. You had it. It was real.

RACHEL   You know what my problem is? I want to belie…I
need to believe in people.

WOLF   Sure. Like the rest of us. You see? You're not alone.
Tell me.

RACHEL   Tell you.

WOLF   Tell me you're not alone. Rachel. I'm not letting you
go 'til I hear you say it.

RACHEL   I'm not alone.

WOLF   Tell me again.

RACHEL   I'm not alone.

WOLF   Good. So? What's the news?

RACHEL   Yes. The news. "In the first formal diplomatic contact
ever between Israel and the PLO, Prime Minister
Yitz"…"Prime Minister Yitzhak Rabin shook hands
with Yasser Arafat. 'Mr. Chairman, on behalf of the
Israeli Government, I welcome you on this occasion
which we hope will lead to peace throughout the
Middle East.'…Mr. Arafat replied, 'I thank you and I
too am hopeful that this will lead to peace.'"…Well.
What do you think, Dad? Do you think this will lead
to peace?

       The End.

Also by Jason Sherman......

Three in the Back, Two in the Head
(Playwrights Canada Press)

Winner of the
1995 Governor General's
Literary Award for Drama.

ISBN 0-88754-534-3 / $11.95

The League of Nathans
(Scirocco Drama)
ISBN 1-896239-15-3 / $12.95

Playwrights Canada Press - New Titles

Mad Boy Chronicle
by Michael O'Brien
ISBN 0-88754-509-2 / $11.95

A lusty, darkly comic, retelling of
the Hamlet story, that *NOW* calls ,
"Wickedly funny...highly theatrical."

The Little Years
by John Mighton
ISBN 0-88754-548-3 / $11.95

From the winner of the Governor
General's Literary Award for Drama,
comes a mesmerising tale that turns
our perceptions of time and its effects on
our relationships upside down and inside out.

This Year, Next Year
by Norah Harding
ISBN 0-88754-546-7 / $11.95

A moving play recreating the love,
courage, and humour needed to keep a
family together as the bombs whistled
overhead in wartime England.

Playwrights Canada Press - New Titles

The Monument
by Colleen Wagner
ISBN 0-88754-507-6 / $11.95

The critic's choice at both Canadian
Stage Company, Toronto and La Mama,
Melbourne, this plays goes to the heart of
man's inhumanity in war time.

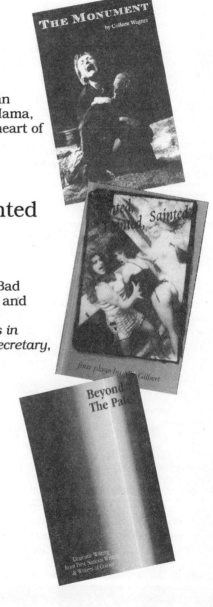

Painted, Tainted, Sainted
Four Plays by Sky Gilbert
ISBN 0-88754-550-5/ $19.95

Plays that established Buddies in Bad
Times Theatre as the premiere gay and
lesbian theatre in North America:
*Drag Queens on Trial, Drag Queens in
Outer Space, Suzie Goo - Private Secretary,*
and *Jim Dandy.*

Beyond the Pale
*Dramatic Writing from
First Nations Writers
& Writers of Colour*
ISBN 0-88754-542-4 / $19.95

25 exciting and innovative
monologues and scenes from
established and emerging
writers from many communities.